By Way of the Heart

By Way of the Heart

The Seasons of Faith

Mark Oakley

CANTERBURY
PRESS
Norwich

© Mark Oakley 2019

First published in 2019 by the Canterbury Press Norwich
Editorial office
3rd Floor, Invicta House
108–114 Golden Lane
London EC1Y 0TG, UK
www.canterburypress.co.uk

Canterbury Press is an imprint of Hymns Ancient & Modern Ltd
(a registered charity)

H
Y Ancient
M &Modern
N
S

Hymns Ancient & Modern® is a registered trademark of
Hymns Ancient & Modern Ltd
13A Hellesdon Park Road, Norwich,
Norfolk NR6 5DR, UK

Permission is acknowledged for reproducing from the Penguin
publication: I Heard God Laughing, Poems of Hope and Joy,
Renderings of Hafiz, copyright 1996 & 2006 by Daniel Ladinsky
and used with his permission.

Scripture quotations are from the New Revised Standard Version of
the Bible, Anglicized Edition, copyright © 1989, 1995 by the Division
of Christian Education of the National Council of the Churches of
Christ in the USA. Used by permission. All rights reserved.

British Library Cataloguing in Publication data

A catalogue record for this book is available
from the British Library

978 1-78622-204-6

Typeset by Regent Typesetting
Printed and bound in Great Britain by
CPI Group (UK) Ltd

For
Dorothy Lewis,
my loving and strong grandmother

Poetry is that
which arrives at the intellect
by way of the heart.

R. S. Thomas

No revelation can be complete and systematic, from the weakness of the human intellect; so far as it is not such, it is mysterious ... The religious truth is neither light nor darkness, but both together; it is like the dim view of a country seen in the twilight, which forms half extricated from the darkness, with broken lines and isolated masses. Revelation, in this way of considering it, is not a revealed system, but consists of a number of detached and incomplete truths belonging to a vast system unrevealed.

John Henry Newman

Contents

CONTENTS

Introduction

Was the pilgrimage
I made to come to my own
self, to learn that in times
like these and for one like me
God will never be plain and
out there, but dark rather and
inexplicable, as though he were in here?
R. S. Thomas, 'Pilgrimages'

On the whole, I'm not sure I like books of sermons. I'm not sure I like this one much either. Sermons are events, not texts, and something inevitably dies when they are printed and read alone. As I look back, though, I recognize that some collections of sermons have been very influential on my thinking about God and the life of faith. I remember as a school boy being captured by Harry Williams' *True Wilderness*, and then, at university, admiring the life-loving collections of Eric James. Since then the sermons of Michael Mayne, Barbara Brown Taylor and Rowan Williams have provoked, excited and changed my perspective with their wisdom and imaginative force.

My own sermons are not in their league. Those published here were mostly preached in St Paul's Cathedral, when I was a Residentiary Canon, although some were preached for special occasions in other churches and cathedrals. The congregations at St Paul's are generally large with many international tourists for whom English is either a second or third language. Each sermon was therefore seeking to be as accessible as possible and not assuming that many in the pews knew the basics of the Christian faith or had any other natural vocabulary for the soul.

Each sermon was delivered in around 12 minutes to a different congregation each time, most of whom I had never met before and who didn't know me. It was a ministry to the general public at St Paul's. This context, as for all preachers, shapes the tone and style of what is preached. I have not edited them to be read as essays. They stand (or fall) as they were written – scripts for a delivery aimed to be heard. As I go back to them, I see occasional repetitions occur as I return to core beliefs that I seem to want to transmit in a particular way. My template for shaping a sermon appears to be 'attract, inform, move'. That is, try to get the listeners' attention and see if they might sense that you are close to them as a human being. John Donne said that he didn't think it was the wit or eloquence of a preacher that won trust in the hearer, but rather their 'nearnesse'. Then after this I try and inform people about something of the Christian faith, the biblical message, an idea or two that might be worthy of reflection. Finally, I aim to see how this might be translated into life and how, if mind and heart have been engaged, our willpower might now need to follow suit. It does not need saying but I will – preachers preach to themselves most of all.

I implied earlier that congregations want interesting sermons to listen to but jokes about the *rigor mortis* of the spouting clergy have been part of British culture for quite some time, usually either 'the bland leading the bland' or about the vicar trying to be trendily informal – and being buttock-clenchingly embarrassing in the process. As an Alan Bennett character says in one of his plays: 'Call me Dick, because that's the sort of vicar I am.' We all know the comedy sketches, from Ronnie Barker to Rowan Atkinson, of the vicar's sermon – showing how a cleric speaking without interruption has been experienced as a comic irrelevance. Fewer people are having this experience as time passes, of course, but research has discovered that one of the top three things that those who do go to church always want from their churchgoing is 'a good sermon'; but, alarmingly, also in the list of the top three things that always disappoint people about going to church is ... the sermon.

Preachers know this, whether they are clergy or lay. At our best we know that we should be thinking through critical questions of scholarship and honesty, being alert to the 'hermeneutic of the congregation' and seeing who is actually wanting to listen to you out there and how their personality types differ so we can adapt our approach. We know we need a self-scrutiny about comfort zones, body language, our fear of certain subjects, and wondering how to preach from our scars and not from our wounds. We know we should think carefully about length, style, variety, wondering if we still have it in us to surprise or try something new. Being busy sometimes seems to stop us engaging with these things as we should, and it can all be pretty exhausting, but when we do, it is a very exciting privilege to be a preacher. Speaking for myself, the process becomes something of a personal adventure because I discover what I believe when drafting my sermon. For me, theology is what happens on the way to the pulpit.

It's important for a Christian, and especially for a Christian communicator, to hold a reverence for words, and, consequently, to be one who loves, celebrates and excites language. I believe in the sacramentality of words. We should be as reverential and attentive to words as we are to the water in the font, and the bread on the altar. Sacraments are about beginnings not ends. The bread of the Eucharist, for instance, is the food that makes us hungrier, making us long all the more for communion with God. So it is with words, full of holy potential and yearning, if we don't treat them as cheap and disposable and if we stay alert to their lifespan in order to wage our war on cliché. Nothing flies over heads as quickly as a churchy cliché. Preachers seek to tune our vocation so that people think and feel in a language in which they have never yet thought but which, when they do, starts to feel homelike. To do this we need to take our words to the gym to get the heart working better. Words of faith should 'quicken', be acrobatic and sprightly. Not dense and dull. Oh dear. I've just written that and now don't want you to read this book.

What I'm trying to say, I think, is that words are not just a medium for conveying something else but sometimes themselves an essential constituent in the experience, and, in the hands of a preacher, the experience of divine presence. Preachers are nothing less than the Church's poets in residence. They are those who dare to break the eloquence of silence by asking, in Bill Brosend's homiletical formula: 'What does the Holy Spirit want to say to these people at this time through these texts?'

There are frightening similarities between the spelling of the words 'devil' and 'drivel'. Drivel used to mean the act of letting mucus flow out from the mouth. Well, we've all had Sundays like that. Language, though, is like water. It goes stagnant if it doesn't move. We are following a man who knew this, celebrating it day after day on mountainsides and lakes, in homes and synagogues. He knew it and we follow him but our own faith and our words may have been sleeping in different bedrooms for a while and to preach is to want them both to fall in love again, spend proper time with each other, explore, be still together, enjoy a playful, serious love and so bring out the best in each other for the glory of God, who at the end of the day is never an object of our knowledge but the cause of all our wonder.

The Welsh poet Dylan Thomas once said in an interview:

I fell in love – that is the only expression I can think of – and am still at the mercy of words, though sometimes now, knowing a little of their behaviour very well, I think I can influence them slightly and have even learned to beat them now and then, which they appear to enjoy. I tumbled for words ... There they were, seemingly lifeless, made only of black and white, but out of them, out of their own being, came love and terror and pity and pain and wonder and all the other vague abstractions that make our ephemeral lives dangerous, great, and bearable. (*New Verse*, 1934)

As I write this, I am more than conscious that this is not an easy time for words. It's been said that the political current in the USA at the moment can be summed up as: 'If you're not at the table, you are probably on the menu.' One of the very evident things about the current administration is its use of language. President Trump campaigned in graffiti and now governs in tweets. With excited talk of 'fake news' we rather get distracted, it is hoped, from fake politicians or populist slogans, generalizations that smooth over, at best, complexity and at worst, the truth. This is not new, of course, it's just particularly bad at the moment – and such abuse, a sort of 'truth decay', spreads across our globe very quickly. It leads to confusion in society about what we believe, what we want and what is possible. Consumerism makes words seductive not truthful, while technology gives us too many words, our care for them decreasing as they proliferate. The first one to draw a breath is declared the listener. George Steiner argues that we are living in the aftermath of the broken covenant between the word and the world. The challenge is that the same doubtful or gullible ears that listen to politicians, sales-people and news commentators are listening to the Christian, to the preacher.

Doris Lessing's novel *Documents Relating to the Senti-mental Agents in the Volyen Empire* is a parable about how

language is debased as an instrument of competitive consumerism and power, words being infected by testosterone
poisoning. Language in Lessing's empire has become so
turgid that citizens often suffer from the condition known
as 'Undulunt Rhetoric', requiring Total Immersion cures in
the 'Hospital for Rhetorical Diseases'. During an attack of
Rhetoric, the victims' eyes glaze over, breathing becomes
heavy, temperatures rise to a fever, and out of the mouth issue
symptoms of intoxication. Both Orwell's 'doublespeak' in
his novel *1984* and W. H. Auden's *New Year Letter*, written
eight years before Orwell's novel, identify this same danger of
language cynically employed where truth becomes as much a
casualty as those who still venture to speak it.

The American poet John Ciardi wrote that 'we are damned
for accepting as the sound a human being makes, the sound
of something else, thereby losing the truth of our own sound'.
Place your ear close up to the shell of humanity and listen.
What do you hear? You can't hear? What's in the way? Other
words, pretending, in stereo. Ciardi abhors language that
removes us from ourselves. It isn't just politicians who learn
such languages alien to the heart, of course; many professions
have a tribal insiders' language that is a sort of conspiracy
against everyone else. I think the present Church of England
suffers from this, employing words and phrases that identify
you as a sound and trustable member, appointable even, part
of the club, but which frankly voiced outside the initiated
circle fail to mean much at all. But these words, sanctioned by
internal sources of power and influence, move in to dominate
the scene, the culture, our conversations, budgets and priorities. They solidify into a check-list vocabulary, the echoes of
which don't reach anywhere much except its own users' distant caves that lie quite a long way from Nazareth and from
our present homes and lives. At worst this can lead to theology being a sort of hobby rather than what it is – survival.
This sort of cold language will always say it is seeking rele-

vance but won't see that it does it at the expense of resonance and therefore is the opposite of the preacher's language, for she looks for resonance in each word and gesture and is very wary of relevance, common sense, the obvious. The preacher must stay true to human experience and avoid at all costs any triumph of the deceptively simple over the honestly complex.

In my book *The Splash of Words*, I tell the story of Tom, a Shropshire shepherd out in the field. Tom's in his eighties and one day he was carrying his shepherd's crook. So I called him over and joked that my boss carried something very similar and then I asked him what it was for. Did he really use it to hook around naughty sheep and pull them back? He laughed. 'No,' he said. 'I'll tell you what this is really good for. I stick it into the ground so deep that I can hold on to it and keep myself so still that eventually the sheep learn to trust me.' It's an important image for the Christian and person of faith – and essential for a Christian communicator. We try to draw on a deeper place, nearer the humus (the root of 'humility'), so that we can be so still, so centred, that we might be found worthy of some trust. For this we need a language worthy of the vocation.

So, in this world of bruised, weaponized, and camouflage language, a time when we can have low expectations of words, we take a deep breath and look for words disengaged from power games and distraction, searching for words that listen, words that hear the pulse, words that read between lines, words that distil, words that distrust first impressions, words from which we can't retreat, words of receptive insight, words without razor blades in them, with no chemical additives but with some natural nutrients, words that help us migrate towards the things that matter, words that dispel illusions without leaving us disillusioned. This language is called preacher's poetry. As R. S. Thomas writes, poetry 'is that which arrives at the intellect by way of the heart', and that sounds about right for the preacher of God's good things.

The English poet Alice Oswald believes that poetry isn't about language but about what happens when language gets impossible. Her poetry, she says, began when she was eight years old: 'I saw the dawn coming up and I realized I couldn't describe it other than in a different language.' As Simeon knew, when the dawn from on high has visited us, people of faith need a language that is richer, broader, deeper and able to resist paraphrase, a language that is not prosaic, that will not lead to lives that are prosaic. When you fall in love you become a poet; some things are far too important to be literalistic about, so we stretch words, phrases, images, metaphors, all to give some expression to the reality. If poetry is the language of love it is the language of the Church. Poetry is not just a set of fancy trimmings to an otherwise obvious truth. It is language brought to its most scorching, most succinct, most pellucid purity, like a Bunsen burner, where we want not an impressive bonfire but a small prick of blue flame that sears and leads us closer into the presence of the holy, the true, the beautiful, the mystery and Source. I believe, though I sadly don't live up to it at all well, that preachers should be poetic. They should be unafraid of providing a fountain of biblical wisdom, images, ideas, images from which to draw and refresh. 'It did not suit God to save his people through logic,' commented St Ambrose.

Up to a point we are socially conditioned against ambivalence, and religious types especially can get freaked out by words not under rational or doctrinal control, prescriptive and literalist. But my point is this: such fundamentalism is to Christianity what painting by numbers is to art. If this bothers you, take it up with the one who taught it to me. 'Jesus came,' says Mark, 'preaching' and he was persistently figurative: parable, metaphor, simile, hyperbole, irony, paradox, sublation, prolepsis, invective and fabrication. The Good Samaritan never existed, there was never a woman who lost a coin, and Lazarus never lay at the rich man's gate – Jesus made them all up. Parables are a way of talking about God by talking about anything but God. I think this has influenced my sermon construction very deeply without me being aware.

Jesus had objectors: 'Can you please tell us what you meant?' Even his disciples pushed him to the point of him getting annoyed with them. But Jesus' style of preaching reminds us that the language of the preacher is not ultimately informative but formative. We have been given our being and what we are asked for is our becoming. God loves us just as we are but loves us so much that he doesn't want us to stay like that. Jesus' preaching is tricky: the words hover over you rather than quickly come into land; they are open to opinions, reflections, different takes. You are where the words go and where they lead you. Pin them down and, butterfly-like, they die.

Jesus' sermons were not preached to make easy sense. They were preached to make you, to remake you, and if we are going to change we first usually have to encounter some difficulty. This is a serious spiritual insight, usually won at cost, but difficulty is important. It's where your full-stops can turn into commas. The most important times in our lives are often the difficult ones. As in life, so in language. We need words that push contours, that interrupt our snoring, help us reimagine ourselves and the world. We need a language that can put the 'odd' back into God. At one point, the Gospels tell us, Jesus told a parable so that people wouldn't understand. I've been tempted to try it out – a nice sermon aimed so that no one can make head or tail of it all, including me – but perhaps I do that every week anyway? I reflect a lot on David Brown's words:

> Fundamental to religious belief is the conviction that, however much the divine has put of itself into the creation, it remains of a fundamentally different order. So, in trying to conceptualize God, words must resort to images and

metaphors that in the nature of the case draw unexpected connections between different aspects of reality, and indeed derive much of their power precisely from the fact that they are unexpected. (*God and Mystery in Words*, p. 20)

An exercise I sometimes do with groups is to say to them 'Here is the News', and watch them sit up and expect to hear the facts of the day, events that have occurred and some commentary on them. But when I then say, 'Once upon a time', they appear to become more involved, equally expectant for truth but tuning in differently and ready to receive it in a different form, a story, where meaning is communicated without summarizing it.

When you walk into a church or a place of worship, how do you tune in your ears? Have you got your newsroom ears on? Have you walked into a Google temple of facts on tap? Or have you walked into a poem? To walk in with expectations of the one and to get the other might mean you miss something very important. It might even mean you think the whole thing implausible. Category errors like this cause a lot of frustration in the brain and heart. And that's why I'm sure Jesus often ended his sermons with 'those who have the ears to hear, hear'. That is, have you tuned in properly? This isn't news, it's the 'good news' and language has gone into a state of emergency to help get us to the place known as the kingdom.

This means that preachers to my mind can relax more about whether they have three simple points, one clear message or 15 well-honed conclusions for everyone to take home or not. The preacher, Jesus-like, can preach of the mystery of God not by resolving it but by deepening it, allowing threads to trail, thoughts to meander, finalities and closures to remain well out of reach, disturbing us into truths rather than congratulating us on reaching a particular one. Meaning can be communicated without defining it – we call it story. Think, too, of the painting in a gallery that though we struggle to understand it, somewhere within we know that it understands us. That's why I feel adventure is in the air when I hear a good sermon.

I can't do all this, by the way. In fact, I'm pretty bad at it. I'm just laying out my aspirations. On good days, I try to remember to strike out every word that's predictable, saggy, dead in the water. Occasionally I dare to use fewer words in hope of better ones and try to leave the listeners expectant, poised. I am happier now to help them see that truth is a questioning place, an ambling landscape, and that while prose is a river you can sail along, poetry and sermons are fountains from which you can draw and be refreshed.

In 1619 Bishop Lancelot Andrewes said in a sermon that our charge is to preach to people 'not what for the present they would hear but what in another day they would wish they had heard'.

So, though I'm really grateful to those who wanted me to publish some of my sermons, now you know why I don't like this book very much.

Mark Oakley
Cambridge, 2019

I

Saving us from Ourselves

stand up and raise your heads, because your
redemption is drawing near
Luke 21.28

When I was at school it was the in thing to joke about un-cool cars, and at that time, the most un-cool car was the Skoda. Now I have to say 'at that time' rather quickly because the Dean of this cathedral owns a Skoda and I know now that they are a superior, high-class car owned by the very best sorts of people. But back then the jokes were relentless: 'How do you double the price of your Skoda? Fill it with petrol.' 'Why do Skodas have heated rear windows? To keep your hands warm when you're pushing it.' 'Why do Skodas come with two spare tyres? So you can cycle home.' And so on.

Over the last few weeks some of us have been wondering again as we read the newspapers whether the Church of England is the Skoda of the religious world. Out-of-date mechanics, a rusty exterior and so clunky no one wants to get in because it doesn't look like you're going to get very far. In fact, you'll probably break down and fall out with the other passengers as to what to do next. 'It's only inertia that keeps us going', one churchwarden once told the Bishop of London. As has been said before, the Church of England can appear to have the engine of an old Skoda but the brakes of a juggernaut.

We could just laugh all this off if that were the only issue. We might just joke about it and move on. But of course, the doubts about the integrity of the Church go much deeper at the moment. Is it just an ageing boys club, full of nods and winks, fearful of women, fearful of bodies and sexuality, of colours and cultures, of difference and diversity? Is it an organization that wants you to fit in rather than belong? It can make you wonder, in its persecution of saints, its rejection of the prophetic, whether it always prefers to be the chaplain to the Empire instead of salt to the earth, the hope of the poor. Is it impaled by self-preservation and hypocrisy? At worst, is it a community where abuse of the vulnerable is almost expected more than a safe place to learn how to relate better, a community that learns to see the world differently with the eyes of Christ and so stands against injustice, the corruption of the institutions and powerful that ruin human lives? Could this yet, realistically, be a worldwide community of people who stand against the indifference that is destroying a beautiful world, against anything that would diminish the dignity of each and every human being? We are very used to a Church that is loyal to the past. Where now is the Church that is loyal to the future?

This Church for the future would be the Church that commits itself to help transforming the world with the priorities of that place Jesus called the kingdom of God, where the reign of selfish empire or religious self-congratulation, with the 'upstairs, downstairs' mentality, their mental and physical cruelties and inequalities, is brought crashing down and the reign of God established. This is the kingdom that you can't get to, you just have to be there. And when I speak of the Church, I'm speaking about me, about you, about us here, sitting at the beginning of a new Christian year, wondering if anything will ever be any different.

So, how badly we need Advent. Advent is the season of the Church's year in the vocative, crying out, reaching out, looking out for help. You hear it in the great 'O's of Advent – O God, O Jesus Christ, O Saviour come, come to us, come and judge us, tell us who we are, who we have become, so we can all admit it and look to be changed. Make us alert so we can stand before you, spiritually naked, ready now to be clothed by something warmer. We are incomplete, come and make whole. We are injured, come and soothe. We are cruel, selfish monsters, come and challenge. We are fractured, come and repair. We are human, make us humane. Come and tell us your promises again so that we can become more promising. Because without you we are our own enemies and will destroy the things we love, even our hearts, our love, our communities and church, our loved ones, our deepest selves.

In Normandy there used to be a tradition on Advent Sunday of paying children to run around the fields and bash the haystacks so that all the rats came out of the reaped harvest. It was a good day to do it. Our rats need taking on if there is to be bread on the table. This season of the Church is not for beginners. It's tough. Advent exposes our darkness, the faults that are usually more forgivable than the ways in which we try and conceal them. Advent tells us to grow up, to face our facts, to stop all the Christian talk of truth for a moment and try instead something much harder – to be honest. In this new light we cry to the sky, and cry out our longing to be made new, to be infused with a new vision, a new story, a new script, a new way of relating. We shout for hope to drop down like rain on a parched humanity, so dry with little ability to grow. Human bodies can often heal themselves. Human souls are not so skilled. They can only be healed from the outside. By love.

You will hear deep in Advent's prayers and music a poetry of yearning and a longing for God to come in our midst and to save us from ourselves. And you will hear, if you listen carefully, an echo, a small voice. It feels holy, sacred, some-where in a chamber of the heart replying to that cry: 'Watch yourself so your heart doesn't get weighed down with worry and distraction so you're trapped. Prepare your straw so that I can be born. And then, when we are together, see how things can heal. I love you as you are but too much for you to stay like that. I love the world, but too much for it to stay like that. I need you: transformation is done together. You, me and everyone of good will. I am coming to you.'

Advent is the season pregnant with God. The birth will inevitably have to be painful. Too much has to change in you, in me, in the heart, in the world, in the workplace, at home and yes, in the Church; too many contours pushed, pasts let go of, securities surrendered, habits broken, all our lives of endless stuff and competitions distilled and brought to their senses, all our insane, mean defences let down if God is to come among us and not be slow. Jesus said, there will be signs, signs of distress, of confusion, of foreboding and fear. How many more signs do we need?

Christian people surely know now we are being called to a renewed trust, a costlier response to grace, a new faithfulness and imagination; no crisis must ever go to waste but be a school for learning how to be more faithful to God's future in us. It has been said that religion is lived by those who fear hell but spirituality is lived by those who have been through hell. Well, it is time for each one of us to stand with our heads up towards the heavens and pray out loud: 'OK. We're ready now, it's time to wake up, here goes – let redemption draw near.'

2

Truth Decay

Pilate asked him, 'What is truth?'
John 18.38

A bishop in the mid-twentieth century, Henry Montgomery Campbell, was known to try his hand at poetry. In his will, it was discovered he had left one of his poems to be read out to all of his clergy on his death. It was short and simply said: 'Tell my priests when I am gone o'er me to shed no tears; for I shall be no deader than they have been for years.'

Well, it is true that not all clergy are fireflies in the dark night of this world. I knew one very grumpy vicar in London who told me his motto in life was, 'Start each day with a smile. Get it over with.' However, the tradition of faith is full of fiery and uncomfortable characters, and thank goodness we still have some today, who are more interested in truth than safety. We tend to call them 'prophets' – people who see the present with an X-ray vision and therefore can see how the future might shape up and then report it all back to us, no matter how uneasy it is to be heard. This Sunday in Advent is the day we often think about such vital women and men.

It might, then, be worth a few thoughts on what is sometimes called today's 'truth decay'. I mentioned this over a noisy lunch the other day to a friend and he, slightly mishearing, thought I would be preaching on the benefits of fluoride. No. I'm wanting to ask whether as a society we are losing interest in truth: the idea of objective truth – facts – now being less important to us than opinions, crisis chatter or infotainment. Is to be interesting more important than being right? Is there a declining value of accuracy, as society's reserve currency? Is what matters not veracity but impact? Is dishonesty therefore not held to account as it once was? Is lying just a laugh that amuses by messing up a system of value?

Now, it is tempting to blame some political and state leaders, if this is our situation. Some seem to think that what is truthful is merely what reinforces the mood of the crowd, even serving us 'alternative facts'. History, thankfully, is peppered with those who warn us about such political manipulation. Alexander Hamilton, for instance, one of America's founding fathers, argued for a system of constitutional checks and balances to guard against the possibility, and I now quote him, 'of a man unprincipled in private life' and 'bold in his temper' one day arising who might 'mount the hobby horse of popularity' and 'flatter and fall in with all the non-sense of the zealots of the day' in order to embarrass the government and 'throw things into confusion that he may ride the storm and direct the whirlwind'. Wow. Imagine that ... Perhaps that's why it was always important to believe that the first President, George Washington, said: 'I cannot tell a lie.'

Those such as George Orwell and Hannah Arendt warned from experience that totalitarian rule ultimately takes hold by slow injections of falsity that people begin to repeat. And so for all practical purposes, Orwell concludes, the lie will have become truth. It spreads and leads to a general distrust of experts, the belief that, say, science, if inconvenient somehow, is a conspiracy, and historical studies that don't back up your arguments can be revised. Journalism begins to reflect a selfie-stick culture, seemingly holding things at an objective distance but actually only reflecting yourself and your tribe at the end of the day. Religion, too, can hide its darker truths with pious religio-speak or some deference to authority and expect the congregations to say 'Amen'. If there is anything to what I say, this is a very dangerous place to find ourselves.

In the Gospel according to St John, Pilate asks Jesus: 'What is truth?', but he doesn't hang around to find out the answer.

After all, the crowd is putting on the pressure outside. A college such as this is built to ask the same question: 'What is truth?', but then to stick around, together, to pursue the answer. A college is one of the antidotes to any fashion of falsity, a group of people committed to the pursuit of truth, in dialogue and fellowship, each ready to be corrected when necessary, passionate about accuracy, fearless in seeing past and present and researching into the as yet unknown. A chapel in a college must be part of this commitment: open, generous, not defensive but a partner, curious for truth. If God is to be welcomed, the paths must be straight, transparent, honest, righteous. I have always suspected that religion works best not when trying to answer questions but when it questions answers. An inclusive chapel community must be as unafraid to reason vigorously as we are as unashamed to adore reverently.

One of the roles of both a college chapel and a church in the street is to remind us that truth has other forms than facts, that sometimes truth is far too important to be literalistic about. The truth that is expressed artistically, musically, in narrative and myth, is the truth that is always part of the human inner landscape. These include the sense of life as fragile gift, the un-ignorable intrusions of mystery when love or loss enter it, the intuition that somehow we need saving from ourselves, from self-destruction, by a love both beyond and within. I believe that when we walk into this chapel we walk into a poem. The liturgy is poetry in motion and we fail to understand its beauty if we miss its density of suggestion, the eavesdropping on the soul, the sensitive state of consciousness that its poetry can prompt. We are not spectators here. We pursue the truths that translate into our living. The truths that transform us are embodied in richly suggestive and provocative, often artistic forms and through receptive insight. They are the truths we learn in authentic human encounter when we dare to take off the masks that work their way into our skin. Primarily, for Christians, to encounter the person of Jesus Christ is the most freeing and freshest truth of all.

Today if we don't stand for something we might fall for anything. Stand for truth. Not even God can work with unreality. Stand, then, for a reverence of language and its proper use. There mustn't be any triumph of the deceptively simple over the honestly complex. As one prophet of recent times, Martin Luther King Jr, said:

> Expediency asks the question, 'Is it politic?'
> Vanity asks the question, 'Is it popular?'
> But, conscience asks the question, 'Is it right?'
> And there comes a time when one must take a position that is neither safe, nor politic, nor popular, but one must take it because one's conscience tells one that it is right.

3

The Reality of Holiness

Herod himself had sent men who arrested John
Mark 6.17

Since his death, John the Baptist has got around a bit. His head is on display in San Silvestro in Rome, and his other head is in St John's Church in Damascus. Amiens Cathedral also has one of his heads and there is a piece of his skull on Mount Athos and another bit in Munich. His right hand, with which he baptized Jesus, was taken to Antioch where once a year it was exposed. If the fingers were open it was to be a bountiful year, and if closed, there would be a poor harvest. A wrist bone is in France, an arm is in Turkey and another right hand is in Montenegro – and one in Greece and another in Bulgaria. It is tempting to agree with Frank Muir that saints are dead sinners who have been dug up and edited.

So, no editing today. We often think of John the Baptist being by a river and forget where the Gospel also tells us he went – prison. He had been put there by Herod, the man Jesus referred to as 'that fox'. John had spoken out against Herod marrying a woman who was both his sister-in-law and his niece.

You might remember the famous story of Herod later condemning John to death. It is a marvellously crafted story of opposites and comparisons. Jesus' followers have just been sent out to travel light, to take no bag or money, just sandals and a staff – that is, to take just what they need to keep moving – and then we are thrown into the great garden party of Herod who has everything, so much he can offer half to a dancing girl. On the one hand, the disciples are learning they have to lose things in life in order to learn what is valuable. John the Baptist is alone in his cell, doomed and helpless but seeing the Messiah for who he is. On the other hand, there at the party we have the successful, the chiefs of state, the military commanders, the leaders and advisers, at leisure and pleasure. We are perpetually and perversely fascinated by the wealth, power, wit and intrigue of Herod's court; many a colourful painting has pictured the scene, yet the significance of the story lies in the death of that starkly simple man in Herod's prison. Often it is those times when we are weak, when we seem to fail, when we understand something of our prisons, that some of the finest, strongest and beautiful details are being painted into our soul's portrait. The Gospel of Mark asks us to look closely at success, belongings and power, the things that make up the kingdom of flaunt and competition, and then to seek the integrity and truth that resist these corrosive acids on our humanity. 'For those who want to save their life will lose it, and those who lose their life for my sake, and for the sake of the gospel, will save it' (Mark 8.35).

Herod, we are told, feared John. He knew he was a righteous and holy person. Fear is often the reaction to holiness because of the transparent reality in its eyes and heart that expose you. Holiness is uncomfortable not because it is mighty and powerful, but because it is real. Herod protected John and liked to listen to him. The seed was being sown. But when he is asked to do a favour for the attractive dancing girl and cut off John's head, Herod is in a difficult place. He had made an oath, his guests heard it and so the cares of the world choked him and the seed and yielded nothing. This may be an ancient story but was one ever more fresh? We all know that a willingness to sacrifice others to maintain honour, prestige and power remains one of the great temptations of authority. It is one of the great temptations of us all – the lie told to cover up an embarrassment, a weakness, a failing; the finger pointed at someone else so eyes are distracted from you; the desire to justify yourself even in your own heart by blaming another unreasonably, even untruthfully. Self-justification is very tiring. The sin of respectable people often reveals itself in flight from responsibility, a reluctance in owning yourself and your actions and facing yourself. This Herod-life we can make for ourselves is the deathly business of shaping ourselves through other people's eyes and not on how God is seeing and loving us. What becomes clear here in this story and then later on as the narrative progresses is that it is not enough just to admire Jesus, to listen, to nod, even to butter him up with fancy prayers and praises. He didn't ask for admirers, he asked for disciples. He didn't ask for people to look at his cross and weep, he asked them to pick up their own and follow him.

This, I'm afraid, is not a religion of therapy, self-help and feeling good. We are offered a cross not a massage. It is a faith that demands something of you, not least loss, courage and sacrifice, the pain of being distilled as we dive deeper nearer God, nearer the real, nearer the true, nearer life as it is meant to be. Today's story reveals that Jesus did not call the qualified but qualifies the called. We are not to be, please God, Facebook friends of Jesus, but apprentices, ready to follow even to the darkest, frightening, alone places that truth and fidelity will take us and that John the Baptist blessed by his presence 2,000 years ago. All the relics we might visit and reverence today must never shadow the stark detail of John's life that tells you all you need to know of true holiness: his prison cell.

4

A Ring on the Doorbell

'Surely I am coming soon.' Amen. Come, Lord Jesus!
Revelation 22.20

'"Surely I am coming soon." Amen. Come, Lord Jesus!'

The words trip off the tongue. All through Advent we pray that Christ will come, that he won't delay, that he will come to us and save us. But is this what we want? Really?

I remember the day I heard Father Gerry Hughes, the author of the excellent *God of Surprises*, imagining a situation today. It went something like this ...

Imagine that, one day, Jesus did come – and came to your house. He rings the doorbell. You are delighted to see him, let him in, offer him a glass of wine and dinner. You phone up your friends to tell them the amazing news. You tell the vicar and the bishop and they invite him to meet the General Synod. Jesus asks to stay with you and you are thrilled – for the first day or two. But then, he starts bringing back people with him, they look a bit dubious, tatty, the sort that your neighbourhood doesn't really like. He was always being criticized for being in the wrong company and you start to see why. He lets these people stay for a while, gives them things, listens to them endlessly, laughs with them, doesn't seem to see in them what you can. Maybe he's a bit naive?

Meanwhile, after a couple of months, your neighbours are beginning to complain about the situation. House prices are falling. They don't want prostitutes, dodgy-looking people, and all those ghastly bankers, tax collectors, and foreigners coming to see this so-called friend of yours. And the Press has turned up because of the things he's said to upset the

Church, the Government, the lawyers, the academics: in fact, anyone with a bit of influence. So, you give a bit of thought to the situation. There's a very nice little room under the stairs that could be done up with expensive wallpaper and some thick carpet. You could put Jesus in there. It would stop him using the rest of the place and spending all this time with his friends. You could put him in the room and, perhaps, lock it, so that he's kept safe – but of course you would ensure that there were always fresh flowers outside his door, and you might play a CD for him, and you could even burn a candle so everyone who comes knows he's there. And Canon Oakley recommended that you should bow very profoundly every time you walk by the little room. Yes. He'll be happy being there, and so will I. It'll be much nicer. But how long will he stay in this little tomb before his love forces itself out again?

We are daring to pray that Christ will come to us, to your life, to mine. Is that what we want? Really? If so, John was right. We'd better brace ourselves: aesthetics were never enough for Jesus. He embraced untidy life not whitewashed tombs. He wants relationships, justice and compassion to be more beautiful than anything that points to him. So, better sweep the stable and work out what must change in us – if, when he comes, it's going to work out together.

Come, Lord Jesus, like rain to parched ground.

5

The Midnight Hour

we have seen his glory
John 1.14

I suspect many of us slightly worry about going to church.
We might think it's going to live down to our low expectations, an excruciating hour on a hard seat when we have to
keep our coat on. Or we might think it's going to be an hour
of irrelevance, sitting in a sort of Wendy House, a place built
for fantasy, made to listen to a worldview that doesn't appear
to match our experience. On top of this you might get a vicar
up in a big box looking down on you who, if not exactly the
bland leading the bland, could be out like a traffic warden
with a headache to slap a ticket of sin on you before you drive
off home irritated. I wonder how many of you had second
thoughts about coming tonight?

But here we all are. Some of us having won our black belt
in Christmas shopping this week, now sitting in a church in
the middle of a cold night. Why? It's a strange thing to do.
Sitting in a dark church in the middle of the night. We have to
ask ourselves, what part of us, what part in us, drew us here
tonight? Then there is that other important question: might
that part of us be our better part?

Something of the draw of Christmas is to try and take
stock of our lives from a different angle from the one we
generally see it from because we know where that usual view
gets us – tired, stressed out, competitive, unethical, jealous,
defensive, distracted – existence of a sort but not living. We
have reached a time when at last we see very clearly that the
circle we have got ourselves into – that circle of spending

money we don't have on things we don't want to impress people we don't like – that circle is in danger of not only diminishing but destroying lives, making us and our planet home equally fragile. And both the anger at this, or the denial that it is so, have the potential to threaten the whole social fabric in their different ways. It was Churchill who reminded us that human beings might make a living by what they earn but they make a life by what they give. The things that matter most, love, relationship, connection, trust, wisdom: these things increase as they are shared. The more you give of these the more you have. They are unlike wealth and power therefore, where if I win, you lose. But all the things that you and I know matter more than anything else – relating, insight, justice – these are founded on the truth that if you win, I win too. That is why before we even begin to ensure, please God, that our economics are ethical, our democracy is fair, we must ensure that our relating and all that makes for a togetherness, a social life – not just a commercial, competitive one – is our unapologetic priority.

But it's difficult. All of us have gone native to a point. And nothing is less self-evident than the self, so self-revision is tough; but we have reached a point when we know that if anything is to change we somehow need to be distilled. We are long overdue for a hard, objective look to see who we have become, and I mean that of all of us: the disinterested need to ask just how indulgent and dangerous will indifference be?

When I conduct weddings I always tell the guests that if they want to celebrate the wedding properly and if they are fortunate enough to be with a partner, then they should by the end of the evening tell them that they love them. If they're English, they usually need about three glasses before this is possible, but human beings can be so deadened by habit, by taking things for granted, by tramline thinking and living, that we fail to see or say what is vital when it is needed, fail to live at some risk to our so-called composure. In all this tightness of spirit so much potential and energy is lost for the cause of good and lives become haunted by what never was. As it is for a person or partnership, so it is for a society.

A large part of the story of Christmas is about a varied group of whacky, fractured people being drawn to a strange place – sheep farmers and magi among them. In a place of austerity, an outhouse in an insignificant town, a spiritual distillation began, an unearthing of soul, a resuscitation. They didn't go to the stable to become more religious, they went to become more human. In that stable, reality is redefined; we see with the clarity of a birth that to be made in this God's image means that a human self will be most itself when not selfish. To be realistic now means very different things from what we first thought. Mary, we are told, treasured what was happening and pondered it in her heart.

In the City of London between 1400 and 1560 it was forbidden to wear masks in the streets at Christmastime. As people made their way home from parties, presumably a little the worse for wear, it was too easy for masked villains to take advantage and rob them of their purses. So masks were outlawed throughout the 12 days of the festive season.

We all have our masks, and some fit very comfortably. The problem is that over time they can begin to eat into our faces, and we become unsure how to remove them. One of the disconcerting but liberating things about learning to love someone, and be loved in return, maybe through the years of a relationship, is that we are shown that we are lovable beneath all these entrenched defences. Love touches us back into life, speaks to us, holds us, so that we retrieve our soul. Love has to be translated through a body like ours that knows us from within, and embraces us in understanding, for it to save us from ourselves and the hurt we can do. By seeing God's glory we begin to understand our own. Words of love must be made flesh if we are to see that masks are not needed if we are to live. It is true that we are fragile and bruised by memory and that we cannot heal ourselves. Only love received from another can begin the repair work and provide the scaffolding to build again. This conventional truth is actually the incarnation in miniature.

The American writer James Baldwin put it like this: 'Love takes off masks that we fear we cannot live without and know we cannot live within.' God unveils, embodies, his love in human form so that humanity can be released from its pride and its fears, distilled in his presence into a soul's awakening. Perhaps the medieval city was right – Christmas is the time to dare to remove our protective, competitive masks. We need distillation. Relationships depend on it. So does all our shared living. Tonight, in the incarnation, God takes off his mask of invisibility and in doing so invites us to do the same. Yes, sitting in a church in the middle of the night. What could be weirder? Sitting in a church in the middle of the night. What could be more important?

6

A Ceremony of Carols

sing the glory of his name
Psalm 66.2

In June 1976, Benjamin Britten was given a life peerage, the first musician to be honoured in this way. He took the title Lord Britten of Aldeburgh. However, by this time Britten was suffering from a heart condition that an earlier operation had not fully cured. He died at The Red House in the early hours of 4 December 1976, 12 days after his 63rd birthday. A burial in Westminster Abbey had been proposed but Britten hadn't wanted that. Instead a grave in the parish churchyard at Aldeburgh was lined with reeds from the marshes at Snape. Inside the church his *Hymn to the Virgin* was sung and the congregation sang hymns from his work *Saint Nicolas*. At the end of his address Leslie Brown, the Bishop of St Edmundsbury and Ipswich, said: 'Ben will like the sound of the trumpets, though he will find it difficult to believe they are sounding for him.'

Britten is rightly acclaimed as one of this country's finest composers. One of the things I admire most about Britten is his talent for engaging words with music, words that you wouldn't necessarily at first think would be made for song. His skill was to allow the music to be true to the language, always keeping the lifeblood, the earthiness, of the words in the music he scored. It all began when he was a boy when he put his favourite poems to music to sing to his family and friends, and throughout his life he continued to bring together text and composition in a unique way, particularly of course for the tenor voice of his life partner Peter Pears.

His *A Ceremony of Carols* is a choral piece in 11 movements that sets medieval spiritual poems, in Middle English, and Tudor poems, within the context of a processional and recessional chanting, as if the story it celebrates is brought into our midst and then taken away beyond reach: the Christian longing for the story of Christ to be within us coupled with the feeling that it feels distant and beyond our capability. Might the trumpets ever really be for us? We sense innocence here before its loss, we sense faith as a cycle of arrival and departure, reverence and rebellion, devotion and dereliction. We are brought face to face with the fragile, temperamental, imperfect people that God comes to in order to save them from themselves.

Britten wrote the *Ceremony* while on a cramped, airless cargo vessel travelling from the United States to England in 1942. Not only did Britten have to battle against the crew's swearing and constant whistling everywhere but this was at the height of the U-boat attacks in the Atlantic. The relaxed joyfulness of the music contrasts somewhat with what was a dangerous journey, precarious and frightening. While stopping in Nova Scotia, Britten had picked up a book of medieval poems and this gave him some of the texts that he set in the *Ceremony*.

Discussion takes place as to why Britten calls this a 'ceremony'. Was he thinking of Yeats' poem 'The Second Coming', which begins:

Turning and turning in the widening gyre
The falcon cannot hear the falconer;
Things fall apart; the centre cannot hold;
Mere anarchy is loosed upon the world,
The blood-dimmed tide is loosed, and everywhere
The ceremony of innocence is drowned;
The best lack all conviction, while the worst
Are full of passionate intensity.

Centres not holding, anarchy unleashed, blood-dimmed tides: the ceremony of innocence is drowned. A world perhaps we recognize, not far away and in need of a procession of innocence restored, a new way of being human to make its way relentlessly into us all if hope is to breathe? This truth is worth singing about. Carols are its celebration.

A message, then, in those simple Latin phrases that hold together the third poem of *A Ceremony of Carols*, 'There is no Rose'. *Res Miranda, Pares forma, Gaudeamus, Transeamus*: 'Marvellous thing, of equal form, let us rejoice, let us cross over and follow'.

7

On the Feast of Stephen

they saw that his face was like the face of an angel
Acts 6.15

Well, the crackers did not disappoint yesterday. The jokes in them were as bad as ever. One seemed relevant for today: 'How does Good King Wenceslaus like his pizza?' Answer: 'Deep pan, crisp and even.' And you'll remember that Good King Wenceslaus looked out on the Feast of Stephen – the day after Christmas Day that honours and celebrates St Stephen.

So, who was he? He was one of the earliest Christians. We don't know much about his life. His Greek name suggests he was a Hellenist, a Jew who had been born in a foreign land and whose native language was Greek. At some point he converts to the Christian 'Way' and is noted by his new brothers and sisters for being 'of good standing, full of the Holy Spirit, wisdom and faith'. Together with six others, the apostles laid hands on him in prayer, ordaining him for a specific task – to be a sort of waiter. His ministry was to distribute food to those in need, especially those whom society thought had little dignity or who lacked support – such as widows. This service of his, in Greek *diakonia*, made him a *diakonos*, a servant or 'deacon'. His was a ministry that imitated the service and humility of Christ. We still ordain deacons today in the Church to remind us all of our vocation to do the same.

One of the early teachers of the Church, Ignatius, told Christians that they should respect deacons as if they were Jesus Christ himself because they imitate his self-emptying compassion, so close to God's heart are they in their calling. I have always noted the fact that as well as the great west doors of this cathedral being opened for the monarch, royalty and the Lord Mayor, they are also opened for those about to be ordained deacon.

But it wasn't his distribution of food that landed Stephen in trouble with the authorities. It was his power of speech. He was charged by the Sanhedrin for blasphemy against God and Moses and for speaking against the Law and the Temple. His challenge to his listeners that they were forever opposing the Holy Spirit, forever blind to the new things that God does and arguing that sin can therefore often be a surprisingly conservative thing – this unsettled his hearers and he was condemned to death by stoning. At the end, he prays for his killers that God will not hold their sin against them. His Christian friends buried him, we are told, with great mourning and sadness. They were burying the first person to give their life for their faith in Jesus Christ. The red that colours the Church today is not that of Father Christmas. It is that of blood.

A bit gruesome, perhaps, for Christmas? Well, in T. S. Eliot's play *Murder in the Cathedral*, Thomas Becket asks in his Christmas sermon: 'Is it an accident, do you think, that the day of Stephen the first martyr follows the day of the birth of Christ? By no means. At Christmas we rejoice and mourn at once. We rejoice at the coming of Christ into the world; but we mourn the cost of his coming: his suffering and that of all who witness to him.' In other words, this feast saves us from sentimentality about Christ, seeing him as a baby yesterday and then trying to infantilize him the rest of the time. No amount of brandy butter can smooth away the cost of that calling in many people's lives. Read of what is happening to our brother and sister Christians in Iraq and other parts of the world at the moment. In fear of their lives because of murdering groups, they are displaced, frightened, bereaved, leaving everything they have. They celebrate Christmas and they understand why this feast of Stephen follows on very quickly.

The word 'martyr' is just Greek for 'witness' and that is what Christ asks all of us to be: people who are willing to pay the price of telling the truth that is in us.

By witnessing I don't mean being pushy. In Scripture the people who really speak for God are usually the opposite: Moses the stammerer; Isaiah who was obsessed with his own unworthiness; Jeremiah who was terminally depressed about everything; Jonah who ran away. None of them wanted to speak. But that was tough. God wanted it.

I think it is the same with most of us. Ninety per cent of clergy and churchgoers are introverts deep down. We prefer a quiet life; we don't like sticking our necks out. But at some time or other God needs us to speak. It might be to explain our faith. It might be to challenge an injustice at work. It might be to defend someone who can't speak for themselves. There are all kinds of situations where witness is required. And with nearly all of us, our sin isn't speaking too soon, it's not speaking at all, because we are scared. There is a worse thing to fear than fear. Fear letting God down. Fear losing your Christian integrity, your soul. Standing in a garage doesn't make you a car. Standing in here doesn't make you a Christian. Your life, faith and courage do.

The Dean of St Albans, Jeffrey John, once said on the radio:

I have a memory from my schooldays that still haunts me. One year we had a boy in our class – I'll call him David. He was a pathetic kid, weedy and rather effeminate. And his life was hell. Children can be incredibly cruel to anyone who's different, and David was a brilliant target. He was beaten up, he got his lunch thrown away, he got called girl's names, and he always sat on his own. I can hardly think of the misery that kid must have gone through. Now I never beat him up, I never called him names; the fact it was happening used to churn my stomach. But I never said or did a thing to help him. Because of course I was terrified that if I did, they'd turn on me too, and I'd get the same treatment. And of course that's how it works, in so many bad situations in the world – and yes, in the Church too. We know what's happening is wrong, but we keep our heads down, and hope someone else will do the martyr bit and face down the bullies with the truth.

Stephen stood up for the hungry, for widows and the vulnerable. He was ordained to reveal the non-negotiable human dignity placed in each of us by God. He stood up for the Christ who had taught him that the defenceless, overlooked and scapegoated are very dear to God's heart. He stood up for the God who had saved him from his self and shown him 'the Way' of being human that did not make fear the last word. He stood up and he witnessed. Now, over to us.

8

Brightest and Best

Then, opening their treasure-chests, they offered him gifts
Matthew 2.11

Epiphany has grabbed the human imagination with great force. Not only are the hymns we sing some of the very best we have, and the art and poetry depicting the magi some of the most striking, but also the traditions of Epiphany are fun – from epiphany cake with its bean and crowns, to the blessing of orchards, and La Befana in Italy. Also, in the East where the Epiphany (which means 'manifestation' or 'revealing') focuses more on the baptism of Christ than on the magi, there is the Epiphany blessing of the waters and boats at which the priest will throw a crucifix into the sea or river and men dive into the freezing waters to find it.

Traditionally on the feast of the Epiphany in the West we think about those enigmatic figures commonly called the 'three kings' or 'wise men'. The Christian imagination has certainly been fascinated by these people for generations, though the story of their travels occurs in only one of the Gospels, that of St Matthew. Although we place crowns on their heads, these *magoi* were outsiders, foreigners, fortune-tellers, suspicious non-Jewish folk with different beliefs – probably from Mesopotamia or what we now know as Iraq, Iran and Saudi Arabia. And Matthew reveals that whereas the establishment, Herod and his cronies, are fighting God's purposes, we see God's new creation, God's refreshing life, expanding through the most unlikely of people – the non-elite and mobile Joseph and Mary, and the Gentile *magoi* (as in the root of the word 'magic'), who were stargazers, horoscope fanatics (a practice condemned by Jewish law). To get a flavour of how they were looked upon you can hear St Paul in Acts say to a *magus* called Elymas: 'You are a child of the devil and an enemy of everything that is right. You are full of deceit and trickery. Will you never stop perverting the ways of the Lord?'

Through the centuries the Christian imagination has been at work. At first the magi were indeed thought of as astrologers (hence their concern with the stars) and were said to have come in droves, not just three (nowhere does it say there were three); they stabilized (if you will excuse the pun) at three no doubt because there were three gifts – one each. No one before Tertullian in the second century thought of the wise men as kings. In the wall paintings of the catacombs and in some Byzantine mosaics the *magoi* wore Mithraic robes. No one actually named them until the ninth century – Balthazar, Melchior and Caspar. This has led to that other Epiphany tradition of marking our doorways with chalk: writing the year with the initials of the magi, CMB, which can also stand for *Christus mansionem benedicat*, 'Christ bless this home'. In Syria, though, they are known as Larvandad, Harmisdas and Gushnasaph. The Venerable Bede suggested that they represented the entire world – one came from Asia, one from Africa and one from Europe – and so one, from the fifteenth century onwards, is often depicted as being black. If you go to the Cathedral at Autun you'll see in stone the three kings tucked up in bed together (the House of Bishops wouldn't approve of that today). They are under a large blanket all wearing their crowns like nightcaps. An angel wakes them and points to the star. One of them has his eyes wide open, one is bleary-eyed and the third is sound asleep – the three spiritual states of humanity.

It was Prudentius in the fourth century who began the business of giving different mystic meanings to the gifts, and you find these in our carols: 'Incense doth their God disclose, gold the King of kings proclaimeth, myrrh his sepulchre fore-shows'. Of course, if they were astrologers and showmen, glittering gold and luscious smoke were probably part of their show. To lay them aside in front of Christ is then more than posh presents. It is laying down one's life and even livelihood built on falsity for the sake of another, better way.

I want to end with a reflection on those gifts, for they might still have resonances for us.

Gold represents our economic interests, as we know only too well. It represents all the things you see about yourself and your values when you look at how you spend your money. A good bit of spiritual stocktaking can be done by looking at your next bank statement. In the case of the magi it might have been the wealth gained by sorcery from the gullible, from those who had no power to help themselves. For many of us it represents a lot of anxiety and worry. For others it represents indulgence, fraud and injustice. It also represents security, home, job. That gold, our gold, is heavy with so much. I wonder how easy it is to leave it with a child and walk away?

Incense may have been part of the magi's magic show, part of their superstition. Incense is traditionally a sign of prayer, always going up to heaven, but like all things with holy potential, like our religious instincts, it can be used as smoke to hide truths, to encourage false piety, to give us a sense of holy security while others are passed by. How easy is it to lay down the apparatus of our faith, the systems and props, in order to worship the true, fresh, living God, spirit and truth?

Myrrh is a preservative of dead bodies. It anoints corpses and things deathly. We all have a side to us that wants to keep everything as it is, to enforce the status quo, to keep life down, as it were. Sin can sometimes be surprisingly con-servative, not allowing the change, the transformation that the Scriptures call the new life of Jesus Christ, to break in to our daily living, into our thoughts and reactions. The

Epiphany was a revelation but it led to a revolution, a turning around of the magi's lives. This is one of the great insights of T. S. Eliot's poem 'The Journey of the Magi'. We translate that they 'paid homage' but the Greek *proskuneo* refers to a posture, a bowing down. It must be the same for us. You cannot glimpse what God was doing in the stable without being changed for the good. Our preservatives must not fossilize us against embracing new, risen life. What goodness has yet to break out of you? What preservative myrrhs will you need to leave at the crib? At the end of the magi episode Matthew writes that they went home by another road – a double meaning perhaps, leaving in a new way, on a different life route now. It was a strange route but it was a going home.

Last year I visited Cologne Cathedral, where the relics of the magi are said to be housed. In fact, they are often referred to as 'the three kings of Cologne'. In medieval days Caspar, Melchior and Balthazar with their mysterious-sounding names were often invoked in prayer for deliverance from evil. They were especially called upon as protectors against the bites from mad dogs or a falling sickness. Most late medieval prayer books have prayers to the three magi.

For me, however, as I sat in Cologne Cathedral I happened to read some words of Siegfried Sassoon written just before he died and I wondered then, as I do today, whether they might have been first thought of by one of the magi:

It has been a long journey, and my last words shall be these – that it is only from the inmost silences of the heart that we know the world for what it is, and ourselves for what the world has made us. (*Sherston's Progress*, p. 280)

'And they left by another road ...'

9

Forget the Birdbath

And when Jesus had been baptized,
just as he came up from the water,
suddenly the heavens were opened to him
Matthew 3.16

I have kept in touch with a few of my teachers from university and some years ago was invited to the 70th birthday party of a professor who taught me New Testament studies. Also at the party was the professor who had taught him in his own university days. The three of us were talking and my teacher said: 'You know, at my age now, you think twice about buying a new suit – how much wear will I get out of it?' To which his former teacher replied: 'Well, at my age you think twice about buying a bunch of green bananas!'

Well, in the Church calendar Jesus has aged very quickly. Only a few days ago, Jesus was a baby in a stable at Epiphany and now he's 30 years old (the age that conferred the right to public activity) and starting his ministry. It's something we don't often remember – that Jesus spent all that time out of the limelight, learning, growing, changing, and presumably slowly developing a sense of purpose and vocation that leads him, eventually, to seek out his cousin at the river for his baptism.

I want to think about this baptism briefly by taking you to three different parts of the world. First, to the south of England, Portsmouth, where in the heartland of the small cathedral we find what looks like an open stone tomb. It is the font. Many fonts were originally tomb-shaped because from the very beginning, baptism was linked to death and to resurrection. Jesus goes down into the depths, the watery grave, and comes up to hear the voice that he is a wanted child, embraced and held for ever. As he comes up the dove is hovering, the same Spirit that hovered over the waters of creation in Genesis, the same dove that confirmed peace to Noah when the waters of the flood receded. Our own baptism is an entering into this mystery of fidelity. The divine love is stronger than the grave and will not let us go, but an old way of living and understanding things has to die before the new life can enter us. On the font in Portsmouth these words are engraved written by St Cyril of Jerusalem: 'When you went down into the water it was like the night and you could see nothing, but when you came up again it was like finding yourself in the day. That one moment was your death and your birth, that saving water was both your grave and your mother.'

Now let's go to the East, to Russia, where the Church celebrates the Baptism of Christ as a sort of preamble to its Easter celebrations. And if we take a look at some of the ancient icons in a Russian church we will find devotional pictures of the scene at the Jordan river, depicting Jesus submerged up to his neck in the water. John stands nearby, gently touching the Messiah's head. Above, a lone dove glides down a ray of heaven-sent light, while on shore, angels wait with ready towels. The icons usually also depict a curious figure. There in the water along with Jesus you can often find a small elderly man carrying a jug. He is the river god, the spirit of the Jordan, the sometime enemy of humankind. This watery sprite reminds viewers that water is not always so friendly. It destroyed the earth in Noah's time. It threatened to swamp the disciples' boat in a storm. It nearly drowned both Peter and Paul. It has a tsunami's power. In one Eastern icon (Ohrid, Yugoslavia, c.1300) Jesus raises his foot to squash this river god. And that's not the only adversary that the Messiah will find in the depths. The waters of the Jordan in these icons are frequented by dragons and great sea serpents. In these icons, when Jesus goes into the river, he goes to do battle against the powers of evil. He goes to confront evil. In other words, by entering the water Jesus takes on our human experience and enters into our chaos, battles, exhaustion, ambiguities – our fights to keep our head above water. Through this, all of us belong to him and he to us. And as we are baptized so we promise to resist what is destructive.

Finally, we go to Rome, to the cathedral church of St John Lateran. If you go to the marvellous baptistery there (a separate room that is used for baptism, to remind you that it is the first stage of a life-long journey) you find enormous octagonal walls that were built to hold a great amount of water, the volume of water needed to wash your regrets and failures off, to cleanse your humanity, to drown all the damaging messages we can transmit to others and ourselves, in order that we might hear the voice of love from heaven. Unfortunately, today you also find there a sort of Italian bathtub of the seventeenth century and across this a wooden plank and on the plank a small bowl with a tiny dish on it in which baptisms are celebrated today. This is a sad reflection of how we can reduce, literally, the way we celebrate baptism and consequently understand baptism. No understanding of a womb-like font here, where nourishment and growth are provided to a soul in development. No sign of a tomb-like font, where we are immersed into the depths and drenched in grace, pushing us down to drown out the noise so we can begin to live up to our God-given name. Just an apologetic pudding bowl or birdbath with a few polite drips of water. I doubt the early Christians would recognize what takes place in the baptistery now. But regardless of the wooden plank, if you look up around the walls of the baptistery, you find words written by St Leo the Great in the fifth century that carry forward to us what began with Jesus being soaked with Jordan water:

Here is born in Spirit-soaked fertility a brood destined for another City, begotten by God's blowing and borne upon this torrent ... reborn in these depths they reach for heaven's realm ... this spring is life that floods the world ... Sinner sink beneath this sacred surf that swallows age and spits up youth. Sinner here scour sin away down to innocence ... but shudder not ... for those born here are holy.

10

Obliged to Twinkle

a light for revelation
Luke 2.32

Our Christian ancestors would have been very excited today. Imagine, in fact, that we are now a congregation, say, 600 years ago. It is 40 days after Christmas and it is the feast known as 'Candlemas', the last great festival of the Christmas cycle before we turn our face towards Lent. We are all excited in that fifteenth-century community although we're also a bit hungry because we were only allowed to eat bread and water yesterday. But today we are looking forward to one of the most elaborate processions of the year, a real celebration when the churches, in the words of a Shropshire monk of the time, 'made great melody', and had done so since the seventh century. It is a day when every parishioner is obliged to carry a candle and to offer it to the priest along with a penny – and after the service big parish feasts were held.

We are going to listen, in Latin, to the Gospel story. Candles aren't mentioned but Christ is announced as the Light to enlighten us all. Before the Mass the blessing of the candles had taken place and the people processed around the church as the words of Simeon were sung. The Mass then began with a verse from Psalm 47: 'We have received your mercy, O God, in the midst of your Temple.' The people's candles would then burn all through the day and night in front of the image of Mary as a sign of the parish's devotion – although we know that in fourteenth-century Friesthorpe in Lincoln-shire an enormous row broke out between the Rector and the parishioners because he had stolen all the candles once they had gone home, presumably for *his* own home. In our electric days, we forget how precious candles were. And all this at the beginning of the month in the year that begins to drive the darkness away from our afternoons – many of the prayers used today contain this image of the retreating darkness.

Not all the candles were left in church by the congregation. People also brought candles to church to be blessed so that they could then take them home. Some churches even had a rotating machine like a chandelier so that each candle was blessed by the priest individually. The candles blessed on Candlemas were thought to have special sacred power, and the prayer of blessing that was said over them suggests this: 'Wherever it shall be lit or set up,' chanted the priest, 'may the devil flee away in fear and trembling with all his ministers, out of those dwellings, and never presume again to disquiet your servants.' People took these candles home to light them during a thunderstorm or when someone was ill; a Candlemas candle was placed in the hands of the dying too: 'Lord, let your servant depart in peace according to your word.' It won't surprise you that people made up imaginative legends about these candles – it was said, for instance, that witches were known to drop wax from the holy candle into the footprints of those they hated, causing their feet to rot off. The misuse of holy things is a dangerous thing. To counter-balance this wild superstition, clergy of the time preached many sermons on how these candles represented Christ – the wax was his body, the wick his soul, and the flame his godhead. The procession in church was an enactment of the journey to Jerusalem by Mary and Joseph to present their child in the Temple.

Now, of course, it's easy to be dismissive of some of this. We can call it superstitious nonsense – lighting a candle during a thunderstorm? What? But it was a different world, unknown, elemental, and raw in many ways. Who wouldn't have wanted to light a candle in a cold dark room with a frightened child scared of the thunder? Making the dying hold a candle wouldn't get through today's health and safety regulations, but in a moving way the loved ones were placing in that weakening hand their hope in Christ and asking the one who faced the journey into death to hold on to that hope, for this was the light for the journey. I think in many ways the laity's taking on the faith of the Church in visual and practical ways is to be applauded. The faith of Sunday morning wove itself into ordinary lives. Research came out recently showing that only 11 per cent of Anglican parents thought it important to pass on their faith to their children through the home. Our ancestors would be very puzzled. What does your faith mean if you don't think it a gift to hand on to those you love most?

The Reformers didn't agree, however. As they focused on the word and on simplification, traditions such as the blessing of candles came to an end. And so in 1548 we are told that the bearing of candles was forbidden throughout the whole city of London – as indeed were other traditions: no ash on Ash Wednesday, no palms on Palm Sunday, and at Whitsun one of the most unusual traditions, that of swinging an enormous censer from the roof of St Paul's Cathedral and releasing doves to represent the Holy Spirit, came to an end. Over time many traditions have returned and I am happy they have. All the important things in life need ritualizing and enacting – love needs a kiss, ideas need art, grief needs a funeral and faith needs a drama, not to cheapen it but to celebrate and explore its richness, its unspeakable truths. Communication occurs on several levels for us sensory beings.

It is easy to see why candles became the focus for today's Gospel. At the heart of the story is an encounter, a meeting, between the old Simeon and the baby Jesus. An old and weary world meets a new, fresh life and the old man says that light has broken in, the curtains are drawn back on a defrosted way of being human. There is great expectancy in the story too – what will it mean for them? But there is also the prediction of pain. The Gospel is bittersweet; it bears witness to the illuminating-concealing nature of God. There is talk of a sword piercing his mother's heart. Life can be hard. Despair can be easy. We cannot afford to take the gift of faith for granted. Lent is coming, says Candlemas; that snowfall in the soul, use it well.

Someone once said of Dirk Bogarde that he wanted to be a star but he resented having to twinkle. Well, there is an obligation in Christian faith to twinkle, to light up and be seen and felt, in a world that can get used to living in a half-light. The candles of today are Christ but they are also to be you: a sign of warmth rather than coldness, of light and honesty rather than deceit and shadow. It is your Christian calling. When the medieval church blessed candles and told people to take them home through the streets and light them at times of fear and journey, I think they understood faith, its warmth, its light to the human fragile soul, only too well.

II

The Untouchable Within

Save me, O God, for the waters have come up to my neck.
I sink in deep mire, where there is no foothold
Psalm 69.1–2

Some of us are a bit 'Jung at heart' and so I want to begin by reminding you of the work of Carl Jung, the great Swiss psychoanalyst who died in 1961. And I want to focus on just one particular aspect of his thought. I want us to look at what he had to say about what he called 'the shadow'.

Now forgive me for being simplistic but I have to be brief. Basically, Jung believed that the human self as it grows up and learns to fit in, socialize and keep people happy (parents, siblings, school mates and teachers, work colleagues and bosses, etc.), the human self develops a 'persona', a mask, a social self or face to present to the outer world like a shop window showing off our best wares. But this persona, says Jung, is that which in reality you are not, but which you yourself – as well as others – think you are. And as we fix this mask on us, in order to be acceptable and fit in with all the expectations around us in day-to-day life, we have to repress, push down, a whole heap of stuff – emotions, qualities, character traits and talents, sides to us, feelings and so on, that are an essential part of who we are but which we don't want seen by others or ourselves. Perhaps they don't go with the mask or we are scared of them because at some time they have been prohibited, forbidden, and we are ashamed of them. We become a guarded version of our own nature and it can feel, in the image of the psalmist, as if life is coming up to our neck.

Just think for the moment about all the forbidden things that may have been forced on you through your life, by others or by yourself. Being forbidden to grow up or change, to be original, to be proud of yourself, to speak your own thoughts, to be alone, to be gay or bisexual without fear or guilt; being forbidden to express strong emotion – fear, anger, tenderness, sadness, vulnerability; being forbidden to enjoy your sexuality; being forbidden to experiment, to not know or feel stupid, forbidden to distinguish yourself creatively, to live the life you dream about; forbidden to feel incompetent or make mistakes; forbidden to have an intimate life, to show affection, to be loved or to love. I could go on and on. Our lives have all these 'don't go there' signs and we push down the emotions, qualities and talents we have concluded are not acceptable. We push them into a big rubbish bag and it gets heavier and heavier. It is our untouchable within – nobody must come near it, including us. It's dark, scary and out of view.

The more we invest in a certain image for ourselves, the more we push parts of us down out of sight, out of consciousness, and this forms what Jung called 'the shadow'. This shadow, or the rubbish bag, can be recognized and explored, often with help, and used for creativity and wholeness, or it can be ignored. Its playground is our dream life. Dreams are where it breaks free and takes some air, sending its messages to us because we aren't taking it seriously. This is why dreams have been thought to be sacred and of God, because they are speaking out of the unseen depths, translating our intimate self to us because our social self has forgotten it. It can be why some people drink or take drugs; layers of inhibition drop away and we start to see the other self that is us, but of course we are not then in a state to integrate what emerges. The thing about the shadow is that it will always come out, whether in our unconscious acts, our projections on to others, our obsessions, unreasonable outbursts or somatic illness.

Depression is its loudest voice. This shadow ticks away like a time bomb in us. 'Whatever we ignore for the sake of ambition,' says Jung, 'will always come back knife in hand to take its revenge.' So, the shadow embodies all the life in us, the emotions, the as yet undeveloped talents that have not been allowed expression. It is not only individuals, thought Jung, that have shadows but nations, communities, groups – and churches (by the way, clergy usually have BIG shadows because of their often very manicured personas).

Jung believed that human beings have an appointment to keep with their shadow, usually around mid-life, the time when one sees that the image we have been working on in life doesn't add up to much and we need to make amendments. As the great mythologist Joseph Campbell once said, 'We spend the first 35 or 40 years of our existence climbing a tall ladder in order to finally reach the top of a building; then, once we're on the roof, we realize it's the wrong building.'

Day to day, one of the most dangerous parts of our shadow life is the projecting we do with it. This is where all the unloved parts of ourselves, which we try in vain to remove from our lives, project themselves on to others, forcing us to recognize them. Those we project on to either become fascinating or repulsive; they are either idealized or loathed depending on whether we feel those things we are transferring on to them are desirable or threatening. Such projection can be very harmful, as relationships become distorted by it we don't relate to the real person but to our created fairground mirror version. 'He hated what he did not have the courage to touch,' says the recent biographer of E. M. Forster. Projection in us or in nations can lead to frightening scapegoating. When Jesus tells us to love our enemies, he asks us to love those who are often bearing the weight of our shadow. He asks us to love others as ourselves, not hate others as ourselves. Indeed, the Gospels are full of stories of Jesus denouncing unhealthy projections, challenging those without sin to cast the first stone. To take back and assume responsibility for your projections will often turn enemies into neighbours. If we don't, we will be affected. As the Hindu proverb says, 'Choose your enemies well because before too long you will become like them.'

So, in Lent we have a spiritual exercise before us – to take our shadow seriously for God's sake. To start to see our shadow will mean such things as examining what we envy or dislike in others and acknowledging those very things in ourselves. It can mean listening to ourselves, especially to the criticism we launch off about other people. So often this is nothing but unrecognized bits of autobiography. If you want to know what a person is really like, listen to what he says about other people. Start with yourself, though. This helps to prevent our blaming or envying others for what we have not done ourselves. By conversing honestly with our shadow, we lift enormous projections of animosity or envy off others, and life becomes freer and richer.

Other windows on to your shadow are such things as asking yourself what you tend to avoid in conversations with people; asking yourself what you think are the most flattering aspects of your social self and then exploring what you have had to repress to achieve this; asking yourself in what situations you become oversensitive, defensive, nervous; in what situations you feel inferior, embarrassed, panicky at the thought of someone seeing your weakness; asking yourself what criticism irritates you, what compliments you can't take. You can ask what value your family most upheld and made the culture of home, and then see what you had to keep hidden. You can analyse your dreams, so often full of dangerous animals and situations, fear and running away (Freud called sleeping the 'undressing of the mind'). You can be attentive to your fantasies and daydreams, your humour and your cruelty. And often at moments of life transitions and conversions, radical changes, we try to forget the past and do a lot of repressing in order to live our new life, usually to later pain, exhaustion or collapse. Your shadow is crying out in so many ways to be befriended. This will not make you perfect, but it will make you complete, integrated, and less tortured. Acknowledging the drives of your shadow means not always obeying them, but owning them. To touch the untouchable within is a road of healing – the whole person, shameful rubbish bag and all, being before God and yourself and those you love and meet each day.

'I'm afraid to tell you who I am, because, if I tell you who I am, you may not like who I am, and it's all that I have.' This is where so many of us are. So, rather than risk being hurt we don't tell others who we are and hide our self, but in hiding it we are in danger of losing it and become a non-self in our relationship to people. To such people Christ spoke, asked their name, touched, lifted up and took the snide comments from the side lines. He comes to the fractured, let down, ashamed, confused, hiding and maybe self-loathing followers of his because he never gives up on us, never abandons us. And what he teaches is that I am because he is. We tell him who we are, light and shadow, because he is the one who will still hold us after we have told him. Whatever road we have been on and are on, he comes too, and his faithfulness encourages us to be our self, to become a true self living and moving in him, to be resurrected and without fear. We can feel as if we have lost him, or he us, but it is his fidelity not ours that is our resurrection. The prodigal son returns with his prepared words, distilled and ready to admit failure. The father is already running down the road, shadow and light all hugged in complete joy because he's home. To look for healing will mean painfully looking into the dark with him, descending into hell, bearing the tension between the shadow and the spotlight, before new life not a false life celebrates a self you can be intimate with again. We have work to do this Lent.

12

The Pancake Life: Fat and Flat

you are dust
Genesis 3.19

Are you happy? Or are you unhappy that I've just asked you
that question? It's a difficult question to answer for many of
us because we don't really warm to that word 'happiness'. It
can sound too sugary and contaminated by self-help gurus
or little yellow faces sent annoyingly in texts. Other terms
for happiness around are equally off-putting, like 'wellness'
which sounds like a town in Norfolk. My dislike of the word
happiness is probably due to its implication that it is a permanent state you can reach if you just try. The word sits there,
rather smugly, saying: 'Here I am, others have found me, why
can't you?' The United States Declaration of Independence
talks of the 'pursuit of happiness' but we know that mere
pursuit of it for itself can be the cause of much unhappiness
and lead us into dangerous places. If you treat happiness as
an end in itself and not something to be enjoyed periodically
while pursuing other ends it can leave us, well, unhappy.

Now, here we are in a church and you might be asking
what's happiness got to do with it anyway? Look at us now
in Lenten array all looking a bit glum. Well, our Christian
ancestors may not have been interested in happiness as a feeling but they were concerned for balance in life. They were
influenced by the ancient Greek thinker Aristotle who thought
that the nearest thing to happiness was the process of trying
to live virtuously and in balance. Virtues for him were those
things that lie between excess and deficiency. To eat is good.
Gluttony is excess and starvation is deficiency. Not good. So

to eat virtuously means a balance between the two. Working with this idea, Christians often saw sins as good things taken to excess. It is good to have self-esteem but vanity becomes the sin and so on. A Christian understanding of happiness became a discovered joy of contemplation about these things, looking beneath the surface, and the delight of this virtue or balance in life. It all sounds a little pious, perhaps, until you think that it is not unlikely that on our deathbed we might wish we had spent more time looking around us and reflecting on the things that matter, and taken a bit more care in how we treated people and the world and sought a better equilibrium in life.

At the heart of Christianity is a belief: God loves us just the way we are but he loves us so much he doesn't want us to stay like that. We believe in two conversions. The first happens when this suddenly makes sense somehow and something inside stirs. The second is that of the rest of one's lifetime, slowly, and painfully, trying to adjust to this different light, a way of being human not yet tried. And so many religious traditions point us to the idea of the journey, the road, the pilgrimage or, for early Christians, the Way. Implied here is that life is not about a search for permanent states or high and pleasing experiences but rather calls us to what we might term spiritual adventure, demanding of us an attention to those inner resources that must deal with change, hurt, the new, the unknown and so on. This demands of us also the insight to understand that we need to be schooled in relationships – for a sense of purpose in life and one's relationships are inseparable. I say 'schooled' (a word that St Benedict used a lot) because today we can think we are in relationship with people when actually what we are doing is assuring ourselves we are not alone. The man I read of recently who had 541 friends on Facebook comes to mind: not one of them knew that he was dead.

It is a very busy world. It is the kind of world that easily consumes us, drains our souls, dries out our hearts, dampens our spirits, and makes living more a series of duties than a kind of joyful mystery. We find ourselves spending life too tired to garden, too distracted to read, too busy to talk, too plagued by people and deadlines to organize our lives, to reflect on our futures, to appreciate our present. We simply go on, day after day after day. Where is what it means to be human in all of that? Where is God in all of that? How shall we ever get the most out of life if life itself is our greatest obstacle to it? Jesus gives us a starting point in the story of the woman caught in adultery. Jesus detaches himself from the confrontation of the righteous mob and the woman. He doesn't bristle and enter into argument. He stoops. He doodles with his finger in the dust. The message here is not that we should opt out of confrontations that may sometimes be necessary but that if we want to see clearly and engage profoundly there are times when we must stoop and refrain. You disengage to clarify and to connect at better depth.

What does this mean for us? Awareness is diminished by overstimulation and unawareness is the root of all evil. Like yesterday's pancakes, our lives can be fat and flat. Our Lent fasting should really be a conscious effort to reduce the mentality called busy, to pull outside of crowd mentalities, to beware of quick judgements, quick cruel words, and, with Christ in the dust, to stoop to clarify and to connect.

Lent is a snowfall in the snow. The air changes. Everything slows down, is heard differently, is seen through a fresh light on the ground. It is a time for you, for a more purposeful reflection, a time that is poised for balance, with so much for you, those in your life, even the world.

'To dust you shall return,' we will hear as a small cross is placed on our head, the place where decisions are made, the place of the human will. That cross is the compass for your future. At the end of my life I hope I will ask myself not 'Was

I happy?' or 'Did I search for happiness properly?' but 'Did I live well?' Did I take time to contemplate this unique little life gifted to me? Did I respond in kind, in some proportion and with kindness? If I can even begin to think that, well, I did try, then I will claim my life and my death to have been happy and I will hold to the hope in Christ that my happiness will turn to joy.

13

Wild Beasts and Angels

*And the Spirit immediately drove him out
into the wilderness.*
Mark 1.12

The story is told of a very holy monk who lived and prayed in the desert. The demons worked hard to tempt him every day but got nowhere with him. One day, as they are recovering from an exhausting day of tempting him, the devil himself came over to ask what the matter was. They told him: 'This holy man won't cave in on anything. We've tried gambling, alcohol, women, men, food, flattery – everything! Nothing works.' The devil smiled and told them to wait there. He walked over to the man and gently whispered into his ear. All of a sudden, the monk jumped up, pulled off the cross around his neck, threw his book down, swore at heaven and stomped off. The demons were amazed. They asked the devil, 'What on earth did you say to him?'

'Oh,' said the devil, 'I just told him his brother had been made the Bishop of Alexandria.'

Well, we all have our limits. Today, as Lent gets under way, we are introduced to that period in Jesus' life in which he began to discover something of himself in the harsh clarity that can be forged in the desert.

We might remember something of Matthew's and Luke's accounts of this time because they spell it out more. Probably like us they are interested in the fact that Jesus was tempted and they want to tell us more. Mark, however, is character-istically brief and speedy. To start with, Mark says that it was the Spirit of God that 'threw' Jesus into the wilderness,

46

a violent verb, kicked, pushed almost. Matthew and Luke changed it to 'led' into the wilderness. But for Mark what is happening is urgent and caught up in divine energy. But, and this is worth reflecting on, God is not leading him into nice easy things. God is leading him into a necessary soul-forming time in a deserted place for 40 days, similar to those 40 years that Israel wandered towards their fulfilment. Translators can never decide whether *peirazo* means 'testing' or 'tempting'. One means checking you are up to it, the other means trying to make you fail. In the Bible God tests to make you grow, Satan tempts to reduce you.

We're not told by Mark what testing Jesus faced but it wasn't a charade, it was what we go through and more, probably, as the harsh reality of the hot desert beat down on his identity, fears and hopes. Silence and aloneness can be very frightening. If you doubt that, just think of all the effort we go to in order to keep them away: the radio in the car, the mobile phone on the beach, the whistle in the dark, muzak in the shop, the bar, the restaurant. And those who live with too much aloneness and quiet can know that you have to be strong to make them fruitful and not destructive.

If we are getting our sense of self only from other people, if we only exist because someone notices us, then we will literally dissolve in the desert. If we get our sense of self from what we own, if what we possess actually possesses us, then our self will collapse in the desert with nothing to hold on to and no one to see it all. If we get our sense of self through an overblown exaggeration of ourselves – 'I am because I am better' – then with no one to compare yourself to, the desert can only challenge you with yourself and you may discover you're not quite what you thought. And in all this subtraction of the self, of the soul, in this simmering pan of the wilderness where so much is reduced down and impurities boiled away, our worth, our dependence and our true possession is rediscovered as the living, holy and eternal God.

To discover this involves much confused pain: wild beasts and angels is the memorable image of Mark. That, perhaps, is a good project for Lent. To spend a little more time in quiet, alone each day, and to work out what the wild beasts in you are that need hunting or taming, and who are the angels that minister to you. Where do you find peace and refreshment, where do you find yourself still growing no matter what your age is? Lent is the time when we should be able to spot wild beasts and angels.

Most of us are not put on earth just to be self-reflective, though. The temptation of Christ follows immediately after the baptism; still wet, he moves into the wilderness. And for us, life after baptism has many trials but the song that was placed into our heart at baptism, the song that our god-parents had to learn so well so they could sing it to us in case we forgot it, that song was God whispering our name and whispering that he would never forget it. 'You are my child. You are my beloved. If you go through deserts remember that name, remember who you are according to me, your creator. Ignore the muzak, live out the song that I have placed there, hear the deeper rhythms, the eternal notes that free you from living to those other deafening distracting tunes that others want you to dance your life to. Face the wild beasts. Hold on to your angels.'

14

Mothering

do not fear, for I am with you
Isaiah 41.10

I have to be honest. Today is one of my least favourite days to preach. It's Mothering Sunday, sometimes called Mother's Day, and it's a day that has always been a bit uncomfortable for me. My parents divorced when I was two years old and my father obtained custody of me and I have never seen my mother since. It's only fairly recently that I've felt able to try and find her but that hasn't come to anything and so the words 'mother' and 'mum' have never really meant much to me. They ring a bit hollow – intriguing but shadowy.

I was very lucky: my grandparents stepped in to help bring me up. Increasingly today, grandparents are the heroes of childcare and so often do a great job in helping to parent and guide children. I was, and am, deeply loved by them – love being the place where all our loose ends find a home.

Thinking of loose ends, it took me a few years to realize what a traumatic thing it is for a child to suddenly find a parent gone. What did you do wrong? Is this a punishment? Will she be back? Who will look after me? These still echo through the years. As we all know, our childhood and formative experiences turn up unexpectedly throughout our lives, the past presenting itself to us and so often in need of recognition. As a pastor I am told I should be a wounded healer but as a human I sometimes feel more like an unhealed wounder.

As we grow up and begin our own life-changing relationships, we also learn the fear or pain of them ending. Who

49

am I if this person goes? Who do I need in order to become more me again? We learn in time how fragile the most important relationships can be, not least when we lose a loved one through death. As I speak there are those who have tragically discovered these things recently in London; the victims of murder are not only the ones who lose their lives. We can bluster our way through life, showing ourselves how busy we are, how in control we are, how we're swimming the waves, but at the end of the day we live first with ourselves, alone, and able to lose as much as we gain.

Into all this beauty and heartache, longing, happiness, intensity, loss, another voice speaks: 'Do not fear. You are precious. I love you. I am with you. I formed and made you. I'm here, and not going anywhere.' It was Isaiah who knew this voice for what it is: the voice of the one who made us and is still making us, still making our hearts, still shaping our souls, because he loves and won't leave, ever. Not even death will get in the way. All our relationships of love in this world, the give and receives of shared love, of partners, family and the dearest of friends, are beautiful and partial reflections of the truest and most immovable love there is. God is the heartland of our very meaning, the source of your life, and is for you, every bit of you, the parts you like, the parts you doubt, the parts you hate. All loved. He's not going anywhere. Love has remarkable things yet to show you. God is mothering us so that we grow in love and confidence.

Isaiah speaks across the centuries. 'Listen,' he says, 'I can hear words, they're being spoken to you out of a heart's deepest depth: do not fear, you are mine, please don't fear, I know it can be hard but I'm here with you. You are very precious. Peace.'

15

Two Bowls of Water

Then he poured water into a basin
and began to wash the disciples' feet
John 13.5

Last week I was leaving St Paul's Cathedral after Evensong when a man stopped me. 'Excuse me,' he said with a heavy accent (I'm not sure where he was from but his English was not very good), 'excuse me, is this a Roman Catholic Church?'

'No,' I said, 'it is Anglican.'

'Anglican?' he repeated, puzzled. He didn't know the word. So I tried helpfully to explain. 'We are not Protestant in that we have no other foundational documents but those of the ancient creeds of the Church but we are not Roman Catholic. We are Catholic but reformed – Established, the Church of England, part of the Anglican Communion, sometimes called Episcopal, and part of the universal Church but not in communion with ...' He looked at me, more and more puzzled, and then stopped me. 'Is this Jesus Christ's?' he asked.

'Yes,' I said, and we laughed loudly together. At last we had found the words for what mattered. 'It's very beautiful,' he said. 'I have said my prayer here.' And he shook my hand.

His question has stayed with me. Is this place Jesus Christ's? Is this church we are in now Jesus Christ's? How can we find out? How can we begin our research in order to answer that question?

Well, one way would be to ask what is at the heart of Jesus to see if it is the same in our heart as a community. Today we see the heart of Christ very clearly.

In the Middle East of Jesus' day, if you were wealthy enough to have a servant or two, when you arrived at your host's for dinner a servant would wash your feet, cleanse them from your journey, make you feel at home, refreshed. And what we find today is that Jesus becomes the servant. It would have been uncomfortable for his friends because it would have been like they were letting him clean their toilet; it was a degrading act for someone to perform this washing. Then, he gives his friends a command that they should do as he has done. This command, by the way, is as strong and as absolute as his command to take bread and wine and remember him by sharing it.

Just imagine if, instead of Communion, the Church had decided to centre the Sunday and daily services around the washing of feet command instead of the bread and wine command. Just imagine what we would have made of it. We would be having arguments over which foot should be washed, right or left (and there would be the Church of the Left Footers and the Communion of Right Footers), we would have synods on whether the water should be cold or hot or, if Anglican, probably lukewarm. We'd be fighting over whether women can wash the feet, whether gay people can have their feet washed, and we would wonder how to behave to those who'd never had a foot washed. We have a clever knack for concentrating on what doesn't matter to hide what does. In that upper room, the clarity is potentially life-changing. 'By this love you have for one another, people will know that you are my disciples.'

Feet are funny things. They are used in adverts to show the size of a foetus. We see them on TV on the slab in murder mystery series when there's a corpse. The poke out of a blanket on a street that's seen a fatality. Somehow they define us. They certainly go where we go. They get tired like us. They get hard, like us. Most people think their feet are ugly. Picking those feet up, he was holding us.

In the Gospels there are two bowls of water in the story of the Passion. One is Pilate's, used to wash his hands of others, scrubbing himself of all responsibility. The other is the one with which Jesus bathes others in love. They are always before us in life, these two bowls, and Jesus shows us that when you place yourself to the side, your soul grows a little bit more. When your self-obsession is reduced, your life enlarges. When you realize that you may have lots to live with but little to live for there is an interruptive call back to living in renewed relationship. People look different from down on the floor by their feet. You look different too. But to pick up the towel is not to become a doormat. We are called to serve not people's wants, but their needs. To serve need in the name of Christ by sharing what we have and who we are.

And after this act he asks them to remember him when they eat and drink. Re-member him – to put him back together, as it were: he's entrusting his future in the world to his friends. He entrusts his future in the world to us. 'Remember me when you come together, become me.'

In that upper room we are shown how you spot a Christian – they love. Is this place Jesus Christ's? The answer is in our hands.

16

Christ was on Rood

'It is finished.'
John 19.30

In the early days of the Church, Christians asked themselves a lot of questions about Jesus' death. Why did it happen? What did it mean? What sort of Messiah is it who gets executed? When you read the New Testament you can see the minds of the early Christians busily working and comparing notes to make sense of the fact that Jesus their Lord was put to death as a common criminal. And nothing changes. Every theologian, every person who sits in church, every Christian, must wonder from time to time as to what the death of Jesus is about, what its meaning is for us today. The interpretations of his death are many and varied. But these interpretations agree on one thing, namely that in some way or other, this death that we remember is an 'at-one-ment' with God. Put those words together and you spell the dense theological word 'atonement'. The many interpretations agree that even though it was at that point that God seemed most distant, most quiet, even absent – it was at that point that his nature was most fully revealed and his love closer to his world than ever. Creation and Creator at one and drawn together some-how by this death.

As Christians reflected on the cross in the New Testament period and over the later centuries, two apparently contrast-ing themes emerged. The first is the glory of the cross and its redeeming work: the cross as the workbench of salvation and the hope of humanity. The second is the pity of the cross, the excruciating suffering, the death penalty given to an innocent man, the heartbreak of his family and friends. As liturgies proceed on Good Friday these two perspectives come in and out of view and, as is often the way in liturgy, we are not asked to decide between them but to sit with both and allow truth to do its work.

No theory of atonement was ever declared to be definitive by the Church. In the creeds we simply hear that Jesus 'suffered under Pontius Pilate, was crucified, dead and buried'. Because of this openness to interpretation and the need to see in the dark, the poets of the world were drawn early on to use their imagination and help excavate some understanding.

The two themes of glory and pity were explored. One of the very earliest Christian poems in English, from the early eighth century, can be seen in runic form carved on a cross in Ruthwell, Dumfriesshire. It has been given the title 'The Dream of the Rood'. 'Rood' was originally the only English word for the instrument of Christ's death. The words 'cross' and 'crucifix' came later and the early English poetic and enigmatic mind was captured by this Rood of Christ.

In the 'Dream' poem, 156 lines long and whose author remains unknown, the narrator describes a strange dream of a wonderful tree covered with gems and he is aware of how wretched he is in comparison. But then he sees that amid all the beautiful stones this tree is stained with blood. The tree then speaks and tells us that it was cut down to bear a criminal but that a young warrior who is Lord of mankind climbed him. The rood is not only vocal but sentient. Gradually a mysterious identity forms between the wood and the warrior, the rood and ruler. The revelatory climax is quickly reached: 'All creation wept, King's fall lamented. Christ was on rood.' The tree speaks not only for the cosmos but as part of it and then charges the narrator to share all that he has seen with others. The vision ends and the man is left with his thoughts, finding himself filled with hope.

The image of Christ in this poem is that of an Anglo-Saxon hero warrior. The poet even uses a native phrase for Christ that is at one point applied to Beowulf. Christ is the young warrior actively stripping himself for the fight, hastening with resolute courage to climb the tree, who then rests 'limb-weary' after the exhaustion of single combat watched over by his faithful followers. By contrast, the cross remembers how it was pierced with dark nails, drenched with blood, endured many grievous wrongs from wicked men, was wounded with weapon-points, stood weeping and was finally levelled to the ground. All the sympathy and pathos of the reader are directed towards the cross itself.

Suffering in this poem is caught up with victory but over what or whom is not spelled out exactly. The impression given is that the victory interprets the suffering but we cannot quite see how. All we do know from the poem is that the Passion is not understood as tragedy but as a fulfilment of a divine purpose. Here is a Lord who does courageously what has to be done. In some early Christian art, this is made evident in depictions of Christ climbing up a ladder on to the cross, freely taking upon himself the cost of a saviour, shown like a fireman going up the steps to the window through which he will end his life. Here Jesus is no helpless victim: he is a warrior hero who, to use contemporary comparisons, is enlisted by God for a cosmic regime change, a man giving his life as an enlisted peacekeeper. We are reminded of the combat that goes into shaping our soul for good or evil. Goodness is fought for. It doesn't just happen. When we hear the words from the cross – 'It is finished' – in this tradition, we sense the battle is over and won.

Thoughts refocused a few centuries later. From the twelfth century onwards such heroic images are less apparent. Instead of Christ the glorious warrior we begin to find an intense meditation on the suffering humanity of Jesus. Medieval piety was characterized by a revolution of feeling, a new interest in a more vulnerable figure of Jesus and his human life and pain. Spiritual writers such as Richard Rolle and Julian of Norwich focus on the bleeding wounds of Jesus as objects for devotion. However, they are not now wounds incidental to a battle but an expression of divine love and pity, which in turn awaken pity and love in the observer. The regal crown of Christ Victorious is replaced by a crown of thorns. The love of the Saviour is fragile in its beauty. People acquainted with wars and the plague see a suffering and death they understand only too well. Christ incarnates their own pain and reveals the nature of God as one who comes alongside. Christ the King is now the Man of Sorrows, his own sadness and theirs. We even start to find carved figures of the wounded Christ detached from the cross, so people were able to focus on his pierced heart and on his five wounds, described in one poem as the 'wound words' that lie on the book of Christ's body that opens up to us the view into God's nature. Now when we hear the words 'It is finished' we think of the tragic, painful end of an innocent life surrounded by those who love him most.

In art, not least in rood screens that were being built, Christ's eyes now close in death, his skin turns white, the blood becomes visible. The Virgin Mary and St John appear for the first time at the foot of the cross, the personal relations of family and friends being brought near to this suffering, making it even more identifiable with. Tears are now a grace, not a disgrace. In this period poetry, music and devotion begin to address the pain of Christ's mother and have direct compassion towards her. Emotionally the poets are so involved with the scene of the crucifixion that they are impelled even to address Mary herself and to compare her pain, her pierced soul, to that of her son. The *Stabat Mater dolorosa* hymn is a good example. This feeling makes the crucifixion seem a contemporary event, a continuously present drama in which we are involved, and it is pity that is the prime emotion. Margery Kempe in her fifteenth-century writing at one point tells Our Lady to cease sorrowing, for her son is out of pain, and she takes her home where she 'made a good caudle of broth to comfort her'. This is devout creativity, praying as though one was bodily present with Jesus' relatives, and it continues today in the poetry of the liturgy of Good Friday, a liturgy that we sense understands us more than we understand it. 'It is finished.' Ours is a liturgy, a faith, a proclamation – of pity and of glory.

17

Playing Chess with God

'I have seen the Lord'
John 20.18

The story is told of a vicar who was not very popular with his congregation. He was short-tempered, narrow-minded, self-righteous and an appalling preacher. Everyone wanted him to go – and kept dropping subtle hints. His answer was always the same: 'When Jesus tells me to go, I shall go.' Another long year passed and things were even worse, his preaching worse than appalling. More hints were given but the answer the same: 'I shall go when Jesus tells me and not before Jesus tells me.' Finally, a day arrived when he mounted the pulpit and everyone settled down as usual for a snooze or tried silently to unwrap a long-lasting sweet, when he suddenly announced that he was leaving the parish the following week. Everyone sat up and the organist suddenly began a hymn – 'What a friend we have in Jesus'!

It's good to hear laughter. And many of our medieval Christian ancestors would have approved. You see, it appears that at Easter Christians were actively encouraged to laugh in church because laughter was the only true way to celebrate resurrection. Jesus had played a joke on death and, though it's said that German humour is no laughing matter, actually it was in parts of Bavaria where a thing called *risus paschalis*, the laughter of Easter, was celebrated. Basically the preacher would try and get the congregation going by telling jokes. Now, those of you who remember Larry Grayson will recall that he used to begin his stage act by coming on and telling us that he didn't feel well; in fact, he said, 'I feel as limp as a vicar's handshake.' Well, clergy jokes, as we painfully know, can be just as limp but it seems that a medieval Easter often saw the priest telling unsophisticated gags, sometimes obscene. I was going to give it a go but as the Dean here knows, I only know clean jokes. But it must have been a bit like 'Carry On Up Your Pulpit' because apparently not all local bishops approved.

Communities would also continue the merriment at Eastertide. Here in England, for instance, we can find activities such as Pace-Egging, Holly-Bussing, Coal-Carrying and Bottle-Kicking. If you went to watch a medieval Mystery Play at the time you would have come across many bawdy characters and a lot of riotous fun as the joy of the history of our salvation was enacted. Churches built at this time often show a lot of playfulness in the architecture and decoration. Diarmaid MacCulloch's marvellous book on the Reformation reminds us of the little country church in Preston Bissett where the priest who celebrated Mass would have looked at a very cheeky pair of buttocks carved under the entrance to the chancel. They had carved a man holding up the arch bent over with the weight on his shoulders, and the priest, as he celebrated Christ's redemption of the human body as well as the soul, was made to look at the equivalent of a builder bending over asking for six sugars. Higher up, equally naughty and provocative things were often sculpted as gargoyles. Again in Bavaria, we know that on the feast of Pentecost a wooden dove was lowered down from a hole in the roof over the congregation. As everyone looked up at it so choirboys chucked buckets of water down through the hole and the member of the congregation who got the most wet was known as the village's Pentecost Bird. The message was clear: the Spirit of God isn't wooden; the Spirit drenches you through.

So, what was going on in these past times, before the Puritans and Roundheads got to work on us all? MacCulloch is clear: 'This was a religion where shouts of laughter as well as roars of rage were common in church,' where the clergy at most waged a very half-hearted battle against fun.

The rock star Mick Jagger and the jazz singer George Melly were reportedly once chatting at a party when Jagger noticed that Melly was staring curiously at his face. 'I know what you're thinking, George,' said Jagger, 'but these aren't wrinkles. They're laughter lines.' Melly put down his drink. 'Mick,' he said, 'nothing's that funny.' I suspect that people tend to look at the Church today and see more wrinkles than laughter lines, sadly. But our forebears knew that laughter is a promise of redemption and faith is trusting that the promise is being kept. Laughter levels, draws people together, reveals our foibles and limits, keeps pomposity in check, hints at something transcendent. It is like resurrection itself. I hope that there will be a court jester employed at the next Lambeth Conference, to keep the bishops in check by bashing them on the head with a balloon from time to time. A bit of 'whoops, there goes my mitre' might be helpful. Laughter helps us become the children that Jesus wanted us to become so we might begin to understand him, might see the world subverted, to see it as God sees it. And yes, it's a serious world but, like Desmond Tutu, we can keep the fight against injustice and oppression alongside a sense of fun and hope, working and standing up against the bullies, so that all can know the joy of shared liberation.

In the resurrection appearances, Jesus does not appear in great glory and hype, like some divine Russell Grant shot from a glitzy cannon on *Strictly Come Dancing* or coming down a heavenly staircase with dry ice. No. He doesn't come to dazzle us but to open our eyes to something. He appears to his disciples in the places he was first with them, the places he spent time with them – the seashore, a garden, an upper room, breaking bread – and says, in effect, 'It was here we were first together, it was here you denied me and left me, but it is here that I am with you again. It is OK.' Our translation says that he saw the disciples and said 'peace be with you', which sounds a bit pious. What he said was 'shalom', which as a day-to-day greeting meant 'hi', 'hello'. So ordinary. 'Yes, we're back together as we were.' He was saying you can rest and live in my faithfulness, you can have a future in my fidelity towards you. Let's start again where we began. Believing that you are lovable enough for someone to say this to you is not always easy. We can hardly believe we are lovable sometimes: the Gospel tells us those disciples were in 'their joy still disbelieving'. To believe in God we can do, but to believe that God believes in us can be harder. That's why today with that 'shalom' we can laugh out loud that we are loved and for always.

The Persian poet Hafiz lived around the same time as Geoffrey Chaucer, and spent most of his life in the cultured garden city of Shiraz. Goethe introduced Hafiz's poems to the West; his work became popular with such diverse figures as Queen Victoria and Nietzsche. Even Sherlock Holmes quotes him from time to time. Hafiz was a Sufi master and his poems express the human experience of divine love. Love is the sole spiritual imperative, the ultimate intoxicant, the only law of the authentic soul. In one poem he writes:

What is the difference
Between your experience of Existence
And that of a saint?

The saint knows
That the spiritual path
Is a sublime chess game with God

And that the Beloved
Has just made such a Fantastic Move

That the saint is now continually
Tripping over Joy
And bursting out in Laughter
And saying, 'I Surrender!'

Whereas, my dear,
I am afraid you still think

You have a thousand serious moves.

For Hafiz, the spiritual life is 'a sublime chess game with God' in which God has always just made a 'fantastic move'. Seeing the pointlessness of all our strategic manoeuvres, and that his one move has defeated any thoughts we might have about defence, we simply burst into a laughter of delight and shout out, 'I surrender!' It is an insight into Christ's resurrection – that ultimately we surrender to God's fidelity towards us, rather than gravely obsessing about our faithfulness towards him. This love of heaven for earth means we can laugh and play on Easter Day without a scrap of Puritan guilt – after all, we are never at our best when on our best behaviour. This is a joyful day, says the Gospels, a day for running away from cemeteries, for eating on the beach, for meeting again over the dinner table, for walking on a road and enjoying the company, for realizing I'm just loved for who I am and not even death will stop that love. No matter how serious a player we think we are, the game is always God's. Alleluia for that! Hafiz tells us that we need to pull out the chair beneath our mind and watch ourselves fall upon God. Nothing, he says, could be more fun. Today we fall upon God in thanks and praise. Alleluia! Christ is risen! He is risen indeed! Alleluia!

18

The Gift of Tears

'why are you weeping?'
John 20.13

OK. I did it. I began Lent as usual with big plans. No meat and no alcohol and more exercise. And there have even been some physical benefits. I've lost a bit of weight. I can now actually fit into this pulpit. And, in fact, a priest of the diocese noticed this on Thursday and said I'd obviously been on the Resurrection diet. I looked at him puzzled. 'The Resurrection diet,' he said, 'you know, three days and the stones just roll away!'

Well, in the resurrection story three days and a stone does indeed roll away. Just what kind of story is this? A made-up tale to stop us worrying about death? A spiritual narrative, like poetry? Or a historical account laying out the facts just as they happened? Well, every preacher knows that if you're preaching to 100 people there are always going to be 100 different sermons being heard – and not one of them is the one you're giving. So with the resurrection story. The richness of John's account means that it has been heard here today in over 2,000 ways, resonating, perplexing, beguiling, inspiriting. I'm sure the author, John, wanted it that way, a rich diverse response.

And today let's not forget something about John and all those who first wrote down these resurrection stories: faithful and imaginative people, those who first shared them, passed them on, put them down on parchment – by doing this they were making themselves, in the world's terms, less powerful, not more. They were walking out into unmapped territory, away from the safe places of political and religious influence, away from traditional religion, at odds with Roman society and the law. They were putting their lives, and those of the people they loved, in danger, at risk of losing everything, even life itself. These stories, for them, were not made-up tales, not something to have on in the background for an hour on Anglican FM on a nice spring morning. These stories were a matter of life and death – and they took the risk, the risk of being the story-keepers, and we thank them.

But why? Why on earth risk so much for a story? Because the story was the best way they knew of sharing an unfamiliar experience they had had and were still living through: an experience that if only they could tell us about it, if they could show its shock to them and its effect on them – an infusion of hope in ordinary complex lives – well, it might just help us too, more than we ever bothered to imagine. This story is nothing less than a glimpse into a new world which they were discovering.

The story is telling. There are tears. Mary is crying. She is there for all of us, for there is so much to weep about. Where do we begin? For the beauty of the world groaning under pollution and plastic, for those whose life will end in parts of the world most of us will never see because they have no food to give up in Lent, they are starving, now. Or will we cry out of fear for a nuclear war between the US and North Korea and where that will take the world; or cry tears of anger for the demise of truth in public debate, tears for those seeking refuge who are more like us than we like to admit, tears for the gay men being rounded up and tortured in Chechnya, and more tears for all the dignity power has diminished and bred fear and executions. Or will it be tears for our own life, the one we have lost, the bed we can't manage to get out of because the day ahead feels unbearable, the tears of the West: having enough to live with but not much to live for? Mary stood weeping. She understands. And tears are a gift. Good things often begin when we let ourselves cry. The question that begins the spiritual life is asked by Jesus: 'Tell me, why are you weeping?'

Upset, Mary seems to want everything as it had been, to take hold of the one she loves, to put everything together as it once was. Again, we understand. 'If only I could be back there, as it used to be, it was all good then.' That's us too. But Jesus is teaching Mary, and us, the next step in the spiritual adventure of life. He teaches us that too often we would rather keep him with us where we are than let him take us where he is going. It is better to let him take hold of us. In other words, if you're serious about your tears, about the hard full-stops in you being turned into commas, then align your life to the journey of an unpredictable God and not to places where you feel safe but half dead. He gave us a prayer to help us: 'thy kingdom come', that is, not 'my kingdom stay'. There will be no resurrection to celebrate if just as he reaches out his hand we bury ourselves rather than him. Unless we dare to let go of who we are we will never become what we might be. It always takes risks to become you. It often hurts before we can hear our own name spoken with love, like Jesus saying her name: 'Mary'.

Her name heard, Mary is given a mission – to go into the city. She is to go into the centre of religious and political life, where decisions are made, where the poor look for help, where neighbours don't know each other so well, where a lot of foreigners pitch up, where you can feel very important or very ignored. And it's there where resurrection faith, the faith that we shout about today, must find its way through. As the poet Gerard Manley Hopkins prayed: 'Let him Easter in us, be a dayspring to the dimness of us.' Breaking open the tombs of human living, shattering the closed doors of people's hopes, smashing down the walls that have made 'us' and 'them', breathing life, a life for all, wherever life has become a system, a masked and compromised existence of heartless, atomized,

THE GIFT OF TEARS

competitive, self-justifying lives. Exhausting. What little can you do in a big city and world in need of serious repair? Well, start resurrecting hope, one person, one relationship, one day at a time. Cynicism is the enemy. I'm always inspired by Martin Luther's comment: 'Even if I knew the world would end tomorrow, I would still plant my little apple tree.'

So, tears in a world of murder and grief. Fear about change or courage for a totally new way of being me and you. Cities and towns longing for fresh vision to arrive – probably in women rather than suited boys. Hmm. And some say this story has no relevance. Nothing could be more urgent. Faith in the resurrection is not a story that we tell to see if people like it or not. As John and those first story-keepers knew, it was a story that was only just beginning, to be continued in you and me. Can we use the gift of tears, and with heart's release follow Jesus Christ as our new compass as we migrate towards a more trustworthy life? And because we now see his love is stronger than darkness, will we fight indifference, cruelty, thoughtless abuse of our resources and each other and power-mad prejudices in the name of God who longs for all creation to be awakened with the new life of his Son? If you believe in Christ's resurrection then it's time to stand up in this faith, out of your tomb, to stand for something, not fall for anything. Or else, what's the point?

I want to end with a story. When I was in the United States in 2015 a young unarmed black man was shot dead by a policeman in Ferguson, Missouri. His name was Michael Brown. A makeshift memorial was built up on the street where he died and there was a cardboard box, painted black but with gold letters written on it. They simply said: 'They tried to bury us. They didn't know we were seeds.' Those words have been used by indigenous people in Mexico and were originally written by a Greek poet marginalized throughout his life: 'You did anything to bury me,' he wrote, 'but you forgot I was a seed.'

Today Christ speaks these words and speaks them still wherever there is oppression. The story is clear. He hugs us with an embrace we don't really deserve but his love is deathless and for us all. Death is dead and hope has taken his place. And so you now are a messenger of resurrection, with a story in your heart. Dry the tears, get ready to renew the purpose of your life, because there's a city and a world out there longing for you to arrive with your strange rumour of God and some notes from a gardener on how to love better; it's a story for which people gave their lives and which began one Sunday with the breeze of an early morning when it was still dark but dawn was beautifully, unstoppably breaking in. The tomb is empty. Make this day the beginning of your new life.

19

First Impressions

I saw a new heaven and a new earth
Revelation 21.1

This time of year is very evocative for me because I was confirmed in the middle of May and I am always taken back to
those who passed on the Christian faith to me, who encouraged me in my first love of God. Some of the clergy who
influenced me were, looking back, in many ways a bit bonkers.
I remember one Sunday morning my slightly eccentric vicar,
after administering communion at the altar, suddenly in full
vestments walked down the aisle and out of the church door.
We then heard him start up his car and drive off. We sat
there, a little embarrassed, not quite knowing what to do,
but being polite Anglicans we didn't say anything. About five
minutes later we heard his car come back at great speed, the
door slammed and he walked up the aisle, still in full vestments. At the altar he said in a loud voice, 'I left the chicken
on high – let us pray.'

'I left the chicken on high – let us pray' sums up in many
ways the life of the Christian. We live in the world, we have
to eat, have to make a living, we get bogged down with the
mundane yet we also live drawn by the magnetism of God's
mystery. We feel the homeland of a kingdom of God which
upturns our day to day; we pray to our Father that his will
might be done here as it is in heaven. I left the chicken on
high. Let us pray.

One of faith's many vocations is not to leave the mundane
and the heavenly polarized, but to see, hear, taste, feel the
beauty of God in the sacrament of the present moment, in

the sacrament of the world gifted to us, in the sacrament of relationships gifted to us – inviting us to see the depth in the surface. Faith is the pursuit of the echoes, footfalls and resonances of the transcendent – within the reality of the universe as in the reality of the self. This means that Christian people need to be very careful, very wary in fact, of first impressions.

For the thing about our first impressions is that they are not 'first'. First impressions (of the world, of things, of others) come out of our past, from all those ingredients that have made us into the person we have become. Jane Austen was originally going to call her novel *Pride and Prejudice* 'First Impressions'. It is our usually camouflaged prejudices that come out to play in our initial impressions and consequently they tell us more about those of us having them than about what or who is being observed. Nothing is less self-evident than the self, and to unsettle our first impressions and what we make of them can be the first attempt at some self-revision.

In the Gospels we are taught time and time again that to live in a world of first impressions is to live a half-life. 'It is because you say you can see that your guilt remains,' Jesus tells the Pharisees at one point in John's Gospel. So much conflict between nations or individuals is caught up with perceptions that are paralysed by the past. And in the resurrection stories, sight and the future are linked very closely and St John later tells us that he sees a new heaven and a new earth and he sees tears being wiped away. The words of Marcel Proust are very applicable to Christian faith: 'the real voyage of discovery consists not in seeing new landscapes but in having new eyes'.

The resurrection accounts in St John's Gospel very much centre around seeing and believing. Seven times we are told that marvellous things were being seen but what's believed is completely wrong. Mary sees the stone rolled away; she believes the body has been stolen. The two disciples see the linen cloths; Peter apparently doesn't believe much as a consequence. Mary sees the angels (or in Greek, messengers), and still believes that someone has taken the body. And then Mary sees Jesus and believes she is seeing the gardener. It's only at the end of this story that at last seeing and believing come together and Mary declares to the disciples, 'I have seen the Lord!' For this she is known as the apostle to the apostles. Once again, the power of this Gospel is not the questions it answers but the questions it asks of us, the way in which it seeks to unravel us, ask of us how we are seeing things at the moment, so that it can then build us up on firmer foundations.

One way that Eastern Christians have invited us to develop eyes of faith is by those windows on to eternity we know as icons. Typically most of the icons of resurrection depict Jesus standing on a precarious-looking bridge. He stands in the middle, and beneath his feet are shattered gates, broken chains and padlocks scattered about. Down in a dark cave you see an ancient Adam and Eve, and Jesus is offering his hands to them and lifting them out of the hole they are in, out of their hell. Richard Rohr says that: 'Religion is for those who fear hell and spirituality is for those who have been through hell.' This is resurrection as liberation – liberation into a new heaven and a new earth. But in some icons it also looks as if Jesus is not only pulling Adam and Eve up but towards each other. Remember that one of the first things Adam does after the fall is blame Eve, and Eve blames the snake. It is as if Jesus liberates them now but also reintroduces them after their blaming match. He dissolves their loneliness by showing us how we are compulsive dividers, compulsive grumblers, and he offers a bridge back to life. Resurrection is here not just a moment of seeing the faithfulness of God's love that searches us out and won't give up on us, it is a moment when human beings are reintroduced to each other across the gulfs they have constructed. This is resurrection as defrosting. It is resurrection as a second look at each other: a second look – not a first impression.

Adam and Eve stand for wherever in the human story fear and refusal of God began. This is a story about the Adam and Eve in each of us, representing where it was we began to forget God. New life, speaks the icon, is generated by the truth that God never forgot you and now wants you to reconnect. So, this means that if you want to celebrate Easter truly then you might need to go home and phone that person you have grown distant from, you might need to write to the person you had a row with, you may need to say sorry to someone, or tell them you love them, you may need to see where winter has taken over your heart and how you have grown prickly, how unhappiness may be spreading through you. All of us today, and I preach to myself, must be careful that we are not Christian in name and atheist in life. He must Easter in us. New ways of seeing something or someone, renewed relationships, to be a little more reckless with our generosity, to trust a little less in our first reactions. Like Adam and Eve, every time we come out of our tombed living we emerge dizzy but whole, dislocatingly human with a sense of a homecoming, with tears ready to be wiped away because the former things have passed away.

20

Put on the Light

While he was blessing them, he withdrew from them
Luke 24.51

The writer Julian Barnes once said in an interview: 'I don't
believe in God. But I do miss him.'

He's not alone. Plenty of people today look around and
conclude that this is a world without God. It's a world
where children are dying in poverty of preventable disease,
people are drowning in the sea trying to escape from war and
tyranny. It's a world where the human heart never seems to
be able to grow up enough to see that the best things in life
are never things, and so we continue to crush each other and
our environment in competitive consumption and take pride
in big things we can launch and destroy everything with –
the final proof of how great we are. And it's a world where
children and parents get murdered in cold blood on a fun
night out with final words never said. Any Christian with
a shred of intelligence will surely understand why so many
are driven to say: 'It all feels like a world without God.' And
perhaps, in secret, for much of the time, that is how it feels
for them too.

In fact, quite a lot of Christian faith is constructed around
experiences of absence. 'If you had been here,' says Martha
to Jesus, 'my brother would not have died.' Later there is his
own cry from the cross as Jesus dies with the question of the
psalms: 'My God, why have you forsaken me?' Even Easter
morning is focused on an empty space and a message that he
is 'not here'. And, in Ascensiontide now, there is the image of
the apostles staring at the sky, seeing Jesus disappear. It used

to be the tradition that on Ascension day the Easter candle was snuffed out, a rather final statement about how the Ascension might be interpreted – it was nice while it lasted but it's over, he's gone now.

Maybe this is one reason why Ascension is often forgotten and not celebrated quite so readily as other feasts: who wants to celebrate being left behind? Who wants a day to remind us of God's absence?

But what those first apostles learned, we are told, is that, yes, they did have to get used to living in the world without Jesus – or at least, living in a world without the Jesus they have known. It's almost as if Christ is saying, 'It's going to be different. Don't expect to see me around in the old way.' According to John's Gospel, Jesus has already told them that it's actually better for them if he goes away. The Gospel of Luke tells us that it was as he withdrew that they were blessed.

One of the great things about the summer is that you don't have that awful experience getting up in the morning when it's still dark of having to turn on the light. For that instant, you see the bulb light up and it blinds you, and then gradually the bulb does its work, you stop looking at it and you start to see everything else by its light. The Gospels teach that it was a similar business with the disciples and Jesus. He first made an impact, they were blinded by him, he was the light of their world, they wanted him to stay, clinging to him, protecting him if necessary. But what they had to learn is that we are liable to hold on to what we can see and understand so as to make ourselves feel safe. When Jesus is just there, part of the furniture, the risk is he will become too familiar, domesticated, a pale, worn-out image of us. Then we can't go anywhere with him. We have to learn to live on our own feet, with the mess of our own hearts and mistakes, but always in and by his light: a spiritual adventure of discovery. In other words, we have to learn what he tells his Father in prayer: 'Now I am no longer in the world, but they are in the world.' He tells them as he leaves: 'You are my witnesses now, my messengers,' and then two men appear and chivvy them along. 'What are you standing here for then? You heard what he said. There's work to do, a world to be woken up.'

The American priest and preacher Barbara Brown Taylor has a husband who is devoted to birds and especially hawks. She tells us that driving down the highways with him can become a test of nerve as he peers up over the steering wheel at the wings of another large bird. Is it an eagle? Or a vulture? He has to know, even if he ends up swerving down the road and running off it occasionally. Barbara yells at him: 'Keep your eyes on the road! I'll buy you a bird book. Actually, I'll buy you a bird. Just watch where you're going.' A few years ago they spent two months apart and she thought she would get a break from hawks, but instead, she says in one of her sermons, as she went out alone she saw them everywhere – spiralling in thermals, wheeling down through the air, elegant in the trees. She says she saw them all for the first time and understood that she wasn't seeing them with her own eyes but with Edward's, her husband's. He wasn't there so she was seeing them for him. He was absent – or was he? He felt as present as ever.

You are my witnesses. Go and see the world through my eyes, love the world through my compassion, stand up for the forgotten with my courage, challenge evil with my anger, make this world through my justice. I'm not going anywhere, says Christ, I'm going *everywhere* – with you, all the way, in you to your deepest self. There will be times when you won't see me, but it's because I must now become the air you breathe, the light you see by, and never an object to pin down – on wood or in mind. It's scary. But as he challenges us to live alone he promises to send some comfort – Spirit, holy, beautiful, just and freeing. And for always.

Jesus hasn't gone away but has gone deeper into the heart of our reality. He is more than a visible friend, he is now the centre of life, the source of energy and of trust. And if people say that this is a world without God, Christians don't say, 'Oh, it's not as bad as all that,' or point to the good bits to cover up the rest. They simply work harder, as he did, in this fractured world to bring hope in the pain we all share in from time to time and which we honestly so often don't understand. Christians pray and speak and listen and behave in ways that bring to light the energy and love at the heart of all things, especially when it feels far away or just a cruel dream. But we know, deep down, that love is the only strength, the only integrity, the only hope, and that hurt will often be its cost.

It's the Ascension truth that it is just when clouds seem to be taking hope from our sight that we are blessed – if we stop looking up at the light and instead look at each other in his light and begin the repair of this world through gifts of compassion and kindness.

21

The Pentecost Bird

All of them were filled with the Holy Spirit
Acts 2.4

As you know, clergy are sometimes asked to say grace at
meals and a few years ago I was asked to say grace at a large
dinner in the Mansion House at which the Queen was present.
It all went well, but as the dinner progressed the woman
sitting two seats down from me got louder and louder and,
to be honest, a little embarrassing. She was obviously a bit
too fond of the bubbly that night – and it got worse. By the
time the speeches were given, she was cackling, shrieking and
screaming with laughter, banging on the table at the not very
funny jokes of the speakers. Everyone looked at the Queen to
see her response. It was, of course, immaculate. We noticed
her just move forward slightly to take a look at the seating
plan on the menu to see who the noticeable guest was. We,
of course, all did the same. You will, perhaps, imagine how I
felt when I saw that the woman – still by the way whooping,
giggling and throwing her arms around her neighbours – was
called 'Mrs Oakley'. No relation – but only I knew that. The
other 300 people were now either looking sympathetically at
me – 'the poor vicar has a wife with a problem' – or silently
urging me to somehow take control of the situation. At the
end of the dinner people gave me hard looks to expose my
cruelty in not taking her home immediately, and making out
that I didn't even know her.

'But others sneered and said: "they are filled with new
wine".' People looked at the disciples of Jesus on the day
of Pentecost and thought they were a bunch of drunks. Of

course, when the Holy Spirit is at work it provokes very different reactions. But Christian people knew that what happened that day was so important that it had to be remembered and celebrated. We know that this Feast of Pentecost, though not as well known as Easter or Christmas, has been celebrated by Christians since the late first century. As the centuries passed the traditions for Pentecost became quite something. Each of them, I believe, says something clear about the Holy Spirit of God.

We know, for instance, that in medieval Bavaria in Germany, they would lower down through the roof of the church a wooden dove, the symbol of the Spirit, hovering over the congregation, to recall the Pentecost story. But the Holy Spirit is not wooden and fixed, no one has observer status when it comes to God's Spirit, so as they lowered the dove, choirboys up in the roof would tip buckets of water down on the congregation to literally drench people with God's Spirit. The one who got most wet was known in the town for the next year as the *Pfingstvogel*, the Pentecost Bird. Now, I thought we'd give this a go … so if you look up you'll see two of our choristers … Not really. Just a bit of Pentecost humour for you.

In other parts of Europe on this day the courts were closed for the season of Pentecost, and servants' work was forbidden. The message was clear: the Spirit sets you free from your prisons and conventions.

In France it was customary to blow trumpets during the service to recall the sound of the mighty wind, the noise of the God you cannot ignore, whose language is that of longing for us, the sound that wakes us up, rallies us. A reminder too that God speaks, not spake.

In England, where the day was known as Whitsun because of the white clothes worn by the people baptized on this day, there were Whitsun ales to drink, obviously in honour of those disciples people thought were tipsy. Horse racing was

the sport of today: the galloping Spirit, carrying us on, jour-
neying with us on our race through time.

In the Oriental churches, congregations had services of genu-
flexion (knee-bending) and poetry, the Spirit making us bend
to his will, showing us what it is like to live as natives not as
tourists in the kingdom of God – poetry and imagination the
only human ways to describe such an indescribable mystery
that is both strange and yet home. Theology, like poetry,
should make no sense if read quickly or with a noisy background.

In Russia, still today even, flowers and supple green branches
will be carried to church – because the Spirit is forever fresh,
full of bud potential, coming to its fullest blossom in the
human heart. St Paul told us how the Spirit flowers in us:
love, joy, peace, patience, kindness, goodness, faithfulness,
gentleness, self-control.

And talking of flowers, in Italy it was the custom to scatter
rose petals from the ceiling of the churches to recall the little
red fiery tongues over the disciples' heads, and so Whitsun in
Italy is called *Pascha rosatum*. The nearest we get is our wearing red vestments, a sign that we are to be clothed with the
Spirit, to catch fire. We say in the Creed, I believe in the Holy
Spirit, the Lord, the giver of Life. Not 'existence' but Life.

Many sermons will remind us that today is the birthday
of the Church, and that is right, but Pentecost is not like a
birthday when we look back. Pentecost is the celebration of
the future, a reminder that no matter how much we in the
Church like to think we are doing the Spirit's work, actually,
God's Spirit is always ahead of the Church, always before us,
willing us to catch up, and that sometimes the Spirit has to
show its work outside the Church so that Christians can be
convinced they need to get moving. 'Such a fast God', writes
the poet R. S. Thomas, 'always before us and leaving as we
arrive.' That day of Pentecost was the day when the apostles
knew that the days of fear and whispering were over. Boats

are safest in the harbour but that isn't what boats are for. The human soul needs its sails to be set ready for the breeze of God to launch us into new lands and places we don't immediately recognize. Spiritually we can become tired not by being led by God but by resisting him, not allowing God to disorient our prejudices or fears. Let sleeping dogmas lie: the Spirit is on the move.

Peter, who preached the first sermon in this new Church founded on Pentecost, took as his text for that sermon the words of Joel: that the young will have visions, the old will dream dreams and people will speak prophetically. This is a celebration and a reminder to us that we are to be a Church that dreams, not in an airy 'castles in the air' sort of way, but in the way that someone who stood in this pulpit 50 years ago, Martin Luther King, dreamed. Dreaming a dream of how life could be, should be, if we really mean what we pray that a new kingdom should be built on earth just as the one in heaven. That Pentecost event says so much: a Church where all languages are spoken so that no one need lose their identity but be included, where they come together, where they speak of God's power not their own. As a Church, to get back in touch with our dreams rather than our dull distractions may be a Spirit-led call to us in our day. We can concentrate too much on the form of the Church and not on what it is for.

So, how will you celebrate Pentecost today? Blow a trumpet? Douse your partner with the garden hose when you get home? Wear that hideous red jumper that you once bought in a radical shopping moment? Get just a bit squiffy on the Babycham? But, not please, if you happen to be called Mrs Oakley. But, yes! Wonderful! Even better, call today on the Spirit of God, that a fire may be kindled in your heart that will defrost what has become cold and cynical, and that you have the necessary courage to face the future with the Holy Spirit, the Lord, the giver of Life.

22

Beyond, Beside, Within

'Holy, holy, holy, the Lord God the Almighty,
who was and is and is to come.'
Revelation 4.8

Nestling next to the National Gallery is one of my favourite places, the National Portrait Gallery. Founded in the mid-nineteenth century, I love walking around and looking at the portraits of the famous and wondering what lies beneath the pose.

So here's a question for you. I wonder how you would like to be caught in a lasting portrait for the gallery? What picture do you have of yourself that you would like others to see? And do you think that picture you have of yourself ties up at all with the picture others have of you? How old would you be in this portrait? Where would you be? What would you be doing? What emotion, position, look would just capture you? What would you like the picture to say about you – 'I'm essentially happy', 'I'm rather serious', 'I used to be thin', 'I love my garden'? What would you want it to hide – 'I've got big ears', 'I am lonely', 'I'm ill'? Would the portrait be incomplete if someone wasn't with you in the portrait? Or would it look at how you are without them? What colours would you want around? Where would the shading be? And then, when you have got this picture just right, would your friends recognize you in it? Would your work colleagues? Would the one you love most? What about those you don't get on with? How painful will it be to hand that picture over to the gallery and know that it will outlive you and that there will be so many things not said in it, thoughts, experiences, feelings not expressed there? After all this, you'll understand why Churchill said he preferred painting landscapes because a tree never complained that he hadn't done it justice.

If you are like me, you will find it hard to answer those questions. We can spend our lives so desperate to be looked at and yet be so terrified of being seen.

Today is the day put aside in the year to look at the portrait of God we call the Trinity. To some extent it is a bit of a self-portrait because we humans can't escape our humanity, our language, our limited brains, and therefore everything we say about God will fail his truth and will reflect our own limitations and prejudices. If triangles believed in God they would probably say he had three sides. That is why the former Archbishop of Canterbury Rowan Williams says that we just continually have to ask ourselves, 'What is the least silly thing we can say about God?' It is why the fire Moses saw can never go out; our silliness has to be endlessly burned away. Yes, in the portrait of God we have you can detect the work of the artists very clearly. And yet, Christian life has taught that this is about the best portrait we have. It is a portrait of God that, like all knowledge of the sitting subject, comes from our lived experience, glimpses of truth, and not from a complete understanding. In fact, what this Trinitarian portrait of God reveals is actually more of God's portrait of us.

Because first, we can say that we are created, willed into being, wanted. Your life is a gift. Your life is an act of reckless generosity to which you are asked to respond with everything you have. Jesus said that we can be so sure of this that we can dare to call this creator 'Father'. For some 'Mother' is better, so nurturing and protective is God, and it gets us away from the idea that God is male – one of those bits of self-portraiture by a historically male-dominated Church. But father, mother: like the good parent God loves until it hurts, allows freedom even if we walk away, suffers when his relationship with us is damaged.

This portrait also teaches you that you are understood, that this creator isn't distant from you but is alongside you, comes to hold you, even to save you from yourself and the damage you inflict on yourself and on others. God has a body language known as Christ. We understand ourselves to be so deeply loved that, like the parent who goes out into the night to search for the child who hasn't come home, God makes us part of his own picture. God made you and then became you in order to understand you and love you from within.

The last part of the divine portrait shows us that God breathes. God the Holy Spirit lives in you and creates community to grow and love in. A portrait of you in isolation is not Christian. We may feel that we are our own best resource and that life is a matter of survival of the fittest, but the Trinity picture shows not only that you are a gift but that you can be a gift as others are to you. It also tells you that you are being upheld at each and every moment and that fresh possibility, creative and life-giving, is the air we breathe when being painted by God. In art the Spirit is often depicted as a dove, warming you, softly breaking your shell so that beautiful things can hatch, relentlessly and gently leading you into your future.

It's difficult in some ways to understand why our Christian forebears spent such a long and argumentative time getting the doctrine of the Trinity in shape. Wars were fought over it. It is not so difficult to understand when we see the human implications of the doctrine, of the picture it holds up to us of human dignity, our origin and future. This is a portrait not so much of who God is, but of how he relates to those he makes. God is beautifully and lovingly beyond, beside and within. This portrait, the best we yet have, shows a complex and beautiful truth to those who gaze on it. God's glory is magnetic, an invitation into mystery, and like arms stretched wide, an outpouring of delight and compassion. Our Christian vocation in response is to look and to love.

23

Believing in Poetry

making your ear attentive to wisdom
and inclining your heart to understanding
Proverbs 2.2

I remember the day I realized my life needed more poetry in it. I went to hear Wendy Cope read some of her poems and towards the end of the session she read this short poem called 'Names'. It is about her grandmother, and as I was brought up by my grandmother I listened carefully.

She was Eliza for a few weeks
When she was a baby –
Eliza Lily. Soon it changed to Lil.

Later she was Miss Steward in the baker's shop
And then 'my love', 'my darling', Mother.

Widowed at thirty, she went back to work
As Mrs Hand. Her daughter grew up,
Married and gave birth

Now she was Nanna. 'Everybody
Calls me Nanna,' she would say to visitors.
And so they did – friends, tradesmen, the doctor.

In the geriatric ward
They used the patients' Christian names.
'Lil,' we said, 'or Nanna,'
But it wasn't in her file
And for those last bewildered weeks
She was Eliza once again.

I listened to those few simple lines that capture the fragile life cycle of a woman you feel tender towards after just 107 words and found I was crying. Not all poems make you cry, of course, far from it, but what became clear to me that day and since then is that when we discuss poetry we are talking about a 'soul-language': a way of crafting words that distils our experience into what feels like a purer truth. This is, I think, what the Irish poet Michael Longley meant when he was asked, 'Where do you get your poems from, where do they come from?' He replied, 'If I knew where poems came from, I'd go and live there.'

'Believing in poetry' can have two immediate meanings. It can mean to trust poetry as a venture, an art, as you might believe in your doctor. This I hold to strongly at the moment. In this Googlesque world where knowledge is thought to be the same thing as information, where we live with the seduction of quick clarity, and where even people of faith are attracted to bumper-sticker theology, honking if it appeals and driving past if it doesn't, in a world restless for quick and easy headline answers, the poets remind us of another, different language. It is not an easy time for words. There are so many of them and they are not reverenced as carriers of meaning but cynically employed now so that everything is possible and nothing is true. So some political leaders talk of 'individuals' rather than 'people', of 'losers', 'swarms' and 'sad' failures all making a world where we see ourselves as competitors not citizens, consumers not communities.

We need a language that is not ultimately about information but about formation, concerned as much with who you are turning into as with what you think you know; we need a language that exposes illusions but doesn't leave you disillusioned. We need a language that places space and silence around things, around words themselves, so that you learn through the disclosure and dislocation of silence to distrust the first impression that is so seasoned with your own prejudice, and enter a distillation process, where the familiar becomes strange and full of intrigue and invitation. To immerse yourself in the scriptures is such a poetic exercise. In the words of Proverbs, they make us attentive to a wisdom. Poetry is, to use the poet Les Murray's term, a 'wholespeak' not a 'narrowspeak'.

Wallace Stevens, a poet I'm drawn to more and more, once said that 'we ought to like poems as children like the snow'. And that air, the stark, clear, striking, warm-chill of poetry where we can see our own breath, as it were, and immerse ourselves in a world reimagined, a truancy from the prosaic and the surface, is why many a priest reaches for the pen or opens the book of poems. Like Celan's image of poetry as 'a message in a bottle' or Graves' notion of it as 'stored magic', poetry promises more of you at the end than at the beginning. It is the language for life's intimate immensities and life's immense intimacies.

And this leads to the second sense of believing in poetry: the believing in God with a poetic sensibility and a poetic language. Indeed, whenever we come into a place such as this we walk into a poem where we hear every time the question of Christ to his followers: have you got the ears to hear? This is not the news now, it is the good news for the soul and the world.

The medieval mystic Meister Eckhart said that God is like a person who while hiding in the dark occasionally coughs and gives himself away. And those who follow the Christian way know that once the initial romance with God is over, the honeymoon, we have to settle into the long relationship, and this, like any partnership, demands patience and not a little resilience. Faith can have a sense of reverence one day and the next day real rebellion, devotion one week, dereliction the next. Revelation both reveals and re-veils; we are always brought back to the mystery of God. Metaphors are the best reminder of that mystery.

St Augustine wrote in a commentary on the first letter of St John:

> The whole life of the good Christian is a holy longing. What you long for, as yet you do not see ... by withholding of the vision God extends the longing, through longing he extends the soul, by extending it he makes room in it ... so let us long, because we are to be filled ... That is our life, to be exercised by longing.

The poets of faith remind us that the heartbeat of faith is longing, a desire for God, and that if we ever think for a moment that we somehow possess God and have captured him then we stop desiring him and the pulse of faith weakens. Faith cannot survive a language of close-down, of black and white, where all is sewn up. The great curse of literalism that prowls around the world at the moment, not least in our churches where it comes out as either ignorance on fire or intelligence on ice, is the enemy of God because God's truth is too important, too enormous and rich and collaged, too transforming, to be literalistic about. Literalism is the opposite of a language of love. See what you find yourself saying when you try and tell someone how you feel when you've fallen for them and you'll see how literalism lets you down. And so it is between God and us. Poetry is the language to which we must turn to begin to give voice to these things. It is an exercise in slow reading so that the heart is quickened by intuition and a doubled awareness that explores the depths rather than just the warm shallows.

24

Who was Paul?

called to be an apostle of Christ Jesus by the will of God
1 Corinthians 1.1

You may have seen that when the British over-50s voted for their favourite joke they chose this one: An elderly woman went to the police station with her next-door neighbour to report that her husband was missing. The policeman asked her for a description. 'Well, he's 35, six foot two, deep dark eyes, black wavy hair, toned athletic build, weighs 12 stone, and is softly spoken.' The next-door neighbour protested: 'Er, your husband is five foot four, chubby, bald and has a loud mouth.' 'Oh ... I know,' said the wife, 'but who wants HIM back?'

It doesn't surprise me that the British went for a joke that sets up the ideal from the reality and laughs at us caught in the tension. The British like a bit of irony and, at best, are fairly pragmatic, knowing that the ideal can often be the enemy of the good. Even the Church has some reticence about rules based on ideals; the Anglican tradition has tended not to ask enquirers to join up by signing on the dotted line but has preferred to hand them a prayer book to see if they'd like to join in. Every strange and weird animal has to budge over on the Anglican ark to give a bit of space to another. It's not a very uniform, ideal ship, but there's a compass and we've set sail nevertheless.

Now, it's sometimes hard to get some uniform view on even the most important thoughts or people within the Christian tradition and this is very true of St Paul. Through-out the generations Paul has been used and abused to back up this theory or that theology. There has been a Catholic Paul, a Protestant Paul, a traditionalist Paul, a radical Paul and so on. Now, again, at its best the Anglican tradition says that when we read the Bible, seeking deep resonance more than passing relevance, we can be unafraid to reason and ask questions as much as we can be unashamed to adore and have questions asked of us. So, what do we think we know about Paul?

Paul was born in Tarsus, Cilicia (modern-day Turkey), around the same time as Jesus but he never met Jesus. Paul began life with a Hebrew name, Saul, because he was of good Jewish stock and would have gone to the synagogue as a boy and learned the traditions and the Law of the Jewish faith. He was taught by an eminent rabbi, Gamaliel, and consequently rose through the ranks himself. One thing we know of Saul at that time is that he disliked Christians – those subversive, troublesome people who had arrived on the scene challenging the religious orthodoxy. He took it upon himself to get rid of them if he could or to persecute them anyway. And then, probably around AD 33, something happened and that something is what we celebrate today. There are three versions of this conversion in the Bible.

We're not sure exactly what happened. In Acts (written by Luke) it is a bright light on a road and a voice; in his own letters Paul refers to a sort of light being switched on in his heart or an understanding he had, given by God. Whatever it was, he changed. More than that, he transformed, from Saul the persecutor of Christians to Paul the influential teacher and missionary who shaped Christianity for all the years that followed him. He was baptized in Damascus and then came to believe he had a special task – to take the message of Christ out of the purely Jewish arena to the non-Jews, the Gentiles. And this is exactly how he spent the next 30 or so years of his life, 'have gospel will travel', establishing and encouraging small Christian communities (churches) across Asia Minor,

Macedonia, Greece, Crete, Cyprus and Rome, hoping to get to Spain, usually in cities.

Fortunately, he wrote letters (usually to infant churches he had founded or visited), and someone collected, edited and published some of them. It is those letters that you still read and listen to today. After Luke's contribution, Paul makes up most of the New Testament with 14 letters attributed to him, although some of them might not actually have been written by him but given his name (for example, Ephesians). His letters are also the oldest part of the New Testament. In those letters you get a good glimpse of the man – full of flash and fire, passion and vigour, wit and charm, pride and humility, enormous self-confidence and fear and trembling. In other words, he was a bag of contradictions, just like us. 'By the grace of God, I am what I am,' he wrote. There's a reference by him to his 'thorn in the flesh' and commentators have got very excited about what that might have been. By the way, people are recorded as saying that he wasn't physically impressive, nor was he a very good public speaker, both of which are enormous encouragements to me.

What is interesting is that he does not tell his correspondents much about the life and teachings of Jesus in his letters. He provides the first written account of the relationship of the Christian to the risen Christ, about what it means to be a Christian and what Christian spirituality might be.

We know about Paul, then, from his own writing but also from Luke's Acts of the Apostles. Paul was probably what we would call middle class, trained for secretarial sort of work. He boasts of being able to work with his hands – rather like some office dads like to say they are good at DIY. He had a trade. He was a tent maker – if you could afford a tent you didn't need to use the public inns that were full of vermin – and he would have travelled around setting up shop, as it were, and probably in his transactions and meetings would have started to talk about his new-found faith. He usually had an assistant with him – and sometimes fell out with them, such as Barnabas. Sometimes he was looked after and given rooms by a patron, and sometimes he found himself in terrible trouble with the authorities for speaking as he did. He got into a lot of scrapes – local silversmiths in Ephesus nearly killed him because he spoke against the idols they were making a living out of, for instance. He was put in jail several times, and whipped. Or as he himself writes: 'toil, hardship, sleepless nights, hunger, thirst, in cold and exposure'. He once escaped trouble by being let down over a wall in a basket (Acts 9.23ff.). However, as he also wrote, nothing could separate him now from the love of God he had discovered in Christ.

It's easy to have a go at Paul. He was a person of his time in many ways: he thought the world was going to end so he had no long-term social programme to change society. He was shaped by his society, as we are, and many of the things that shaped him no longer shape us; in fact, we find some of them unpleasant or wrong – not many women cover their heads when they come to church today, for instance. But at the heart of what Paul was saying was something rather radical. He said he was not eloquent but he was preaching God's wisdom – which sounds foolish. He said his weaknesses were his strengths because that's where God helped him and pushed him most. 'When I am weak, then I am strong.' He preached a God for whom 'there is neither Jew, nor Greek, neither slave nor free, neither male nor female, for you are all one in Christ Jesus.' He wanted a Church that was the body of Christ, where people worked hard to get on together, where if one member suffers all suffer, where the less respectable are given the most honour. We are ambassadors for Christ. He knew that there are three things that last for ever: faith, hope and love, and the greatest of these is love. He passionately believed that if anyone was in Christ there is a new creation. He knew that nothing we do can ever earn God's love; you can't buy favour by religion, ethics or anything else. It is only

God and his grace that can pick us up and restore us back to a wholeness and that though our outward nature is wasting away, our inward selves are renewed every day by him. Christ the risen one was a resurrector. He also knew that he wasn't finished: 'forgetting what lies behind and straining forward to what lies ahead, I press on towards the goal for the prize of the heavenly call of God in Christ Jesus.'

Christians in Jerusalem needed money (nothing changes) and Paul took collections from his churches in other places and decided to deliver it personally at great danger to himself. It was a practical sign that the Church was a unity. He had enemies, was accused of taking a Gentile into the Temple, was imprisoned, and eventually sent to Rome for trial. It appears he was then executed by having his head severed or as part of the general persecution of Christians by Nero – a hideous suffering for Christian faith that makes me in my complacency blush.

With this knowledge you can hear his words differently. Hear him, bloodied and bruised, sitting in his dark cell painfully writing: 'Who shall separate us from the love of Christ, shall tribulation, or distress, or persecution, or famine, or nakedness, or peril, or sword? No, in all these things we are more than conquerors through him who loved us. For I am sure that neither death, nor life, nor things past nor things to come, nor anything else in all creation will be able to separate us from the love of God in Christ Jesus our Lord.'

And that's why we remember him – because for some of us it takes a lifetime to see it, to believe it. But Paul knew it deep in his heart – to the very end – and left as his legacy those simple words of his letter to the Colossians: 'I want your hearts to be encouraged and united in love so that you may have knowledge of God's mystery, Christ himself, in whom are hidden all the treasures.'

Blessed Paul, servant of Christ, we acclaim you and thank you!

25

Be Bold Therefore

Let the word of Christ dwell in you richly
Colossians 3.16

When I left St John's Wood Church at the end of my curacy at the age of 27, it was to become Chaplain to the new Bishop of London, Richard Chartres. It's a strange job, as I was to find out. You're a sort of mixture of lady-in-waiting, always having necessities to hand, Alastair Campbell, helping to draft papers and interpret your boss to the public, and Mr Slope of Barchester, keeping your ear to the ground to ensure the bishop isn't caught out. The chaplain also processes behind the bishop in services, which means that you can often hear comments from the pews as you walk by. I remember one Christmas in St Paul's, with the Bishop in a very sparkly cope and all six foot three of him with a very large mitre on top, in candlelight and surrounded by incense, holding his crozier. A rather flamboyant and well-known actor was sitting at the front and as we walked by he turned to his friend: 'Darling!' he said, looking at the Bishop, 'VERY Darth Vader!'

Let me tell you about another procession in St Paul's; this time it was not made up of bishops or choirs but of the general public. It wormed its way around the cathedral and led to a glass case. In the case was a very small book. You might almost miss it but 1,600 people made sure that they didn't. This book, you see, was a New Testament and the reason it is so small is so that it could be easily hidden, because when it was made if you were found in possession of this book or one like it you would most likely have been tortured or even killed. Why? Because it was in English. It had, with a few thousand others, been published in Cologne and smuggled into England up the Thames in cargo boats, stashed away in stores of cloth and wine. The translator of this English testament was a Gloucestershire man called William Tyndale. He had always wanted to translate the Bible from its original languages into the language of his people, the English, just as Luther had done for the Germans. He wanted, he once said, a simple ploughboy to end up knowing the Scriptures better than the Pope, by having them available to him, in his pocket, in his own language and not in Latin.

To make the Bible accessible in this way, outside of the control of the Church or state, was deemed by such as the then Bishop of London, Bishop Tunstall, to be 'pernicious, pestilent, heretical and contaminating', and so the Bishop bought up as many copies as he could lay his hands on and on 27 October 1526 burned them all on a bonfire outside St Paul's. King Henry VIII approved, calling Tyndale the most dangerous man in England. And that is why he had to go into hiding abroad. It is also why there are only three surviving copies of Tyndale's New Testament left in the world today and St Paul's is privileged to own one of them.

Eventually, Tyndale was hunted down abroad and put in prison and then led to the stake where he was strangled – but not killed – and then burned to death. His last prayer, it is said, was: 'O Lord, open the King of England's eyes'. Then, say onlookers, this great man of language, the lover of words and the proclamation of the gospel, kept complete silence as the flames did their work on him. His prayer was answered. Within three years, Henry had changed his mind and an English copy of the Bible was placed into every parish church.

Tyndale is, in many ways, rather forgotten. And yet his scholarship, courage and determined faith has been hugely influential and has a strong legacy – not least in the famous and much loved King James Bible, which was published only

75 years after Tyndale's death in 1611. Although Tyndale doesn't get a mention it is estimated that 93 per cent of the King James New Testament is cribbed directly from Tyndale. Likewise more than 85 per cent of five key books of the Old Testament are also his work. He often chose words that were monosyllabic, punchy and easy to remember for the illiterate who heard it read out loud. And if you're wondering what sort of words he chose, here are a few: 'see the writing on the wall', 'cast the first stone', 'the salt of the earth', 'a thorn in the flesh', 'fight the good fight', 'from strength to strength', 'the blind lead the blind', 'sick unto death', 'broken-hearted', 'clear eyed', 'the powers that be'. And then there is the Lord's Prayer and the Beatitudes whose rhythms still translate their truths into our lives and hearts.

Any anniversary of the Reformation can focus mainly on Luther and for good reasons. But let's not forget William Tyndale, the man who gave us the Scriptures in our language and co-created modern English in the process. We are those who benefit from his deepest belief that, in his words, 'the sun itself is not more common and open to all than the teaching of Christ', and that those words that will never pass away must be available and free to all who are searching.

I started with Richard Chartres and then we met Bishop Cuthbert Tunstall, book burner extraordinaire. Future Bishops of London will also have the legacy of Tyndale to live with in trying to keep his or her flock together in love because, of course, as the Bible became accessible so the interpretation of it became disputed, and nothing perhaps divides Christians so much as their different approaches to the Bible. This ranges from those who see it as the completely inerrant, divinely inspired Word of God, factually and historically to be read literally, to those, like me, who think that such fundamentalism is to Christianity what painting by numbers is to art, and that the Bible is a majestic, confusing, often challenging and often comforting collage, but a true voice approaching the reality and mystery of God. Its glory is that it doesn't always answer our questions so much as question our answers. It reminds us not to make God a mere bigger version of ourselves and to ensure we put the odd back into God. Tyndale reminded his people that 'Christ is with us until the world's end. Let his little flock be bold therefore.'

Two final thoughts on this Bible Sunday. The first is that ultimately the Bible is not there so much to be informative as to be formative. The Bible is there to help you tune yourself and your life to heaven's humility and not to feel good about getting everything right. It is heart-knowledge, wisdom, distilling often by difficulty. As Paul says, it is a word that is to dwell in us richly. The second thought is one passed on by an early Church theologian who said that when we read the Bible as Christians, better together than alone, we ought not to hammer to death a word or a phrase but to treat the whole as a letter from a friend and therefore to read the love between the lines. And if, he continued, you cannot hear the love between the lines of Scripture as someone is interpreting it to you, be very aware: it's not to be trusted. This was also the thought of St Augustine:

> Whoever, then, thinks that he understands the Holy Scriptures, or any part of them, but puts such an interpretation upon them as does not tend to build up this twofold love of God and our neighbour, does not yet understand them as he ought.

Tyndale, though, must have the final words. Exiled, tormented, ridiculed, imprisoned, incinerated for the words we can so take for granted – this man sought to translate the gospel hope into his life. He wrote:

> Evangelion (that we call the Gospel) is a Greek word and signifieth good, merry, glad and joyful tidings, that maketh

a man's heart glad and maketh him sing, dance and leap for joy.

Be bold, little flock. Be bold.

May he dance and leap in that joy now in the presence of our God for ever.

26

A Saint for Our Day

Fight the good fight of the faith
1 Timothy 6.12

One summer when I was in San Francisco I visited the church of St Gregory of Nyssa. Inside the church around the walls are painted icons of 100 saints and friends of God's justice. They are not all Christian and some are surprising. They range from Dante to Anne Frank, from Malcom X to William Byrd, from Ella Fitzgerald to Mary Magdalene: and they are linked up in a great dance together, dancing in tune with heaven and each other. All of them have halos except one – Desmond Mpilo Tutu. This is not because he's not as holy as the others. It's because he is the only saint depicted on the walls there who is still alive. He's there already. It's as if, and if you know him you'll know how this is believable, he couldn't stay out of the dance. He had to get on the floor, join in and get down. He loves a party. He is a firefly, with a volcano for a soul, a whirl of energy that, when it comes into the room, you don't quite know what's hit you.

In his eighties now, Tutu is retired but like a helium balloon it's hard to keep him down. His is an extraordinary life. Born in the Transvaal in the apartheid era to a teacher and a cook, his family moved to Johannesburg and it was here that he met Trevor Huddleston who was at the time a parish priest in the black slum of Sophiatown. 'One day,' says Tutu, 'I was standing in the street with my mother when a white man in a priest's clothing walked past. As he passed he took off his hat to my mother. I couldn't believe my eyes – a white man who greeted a black working-class woman!'

Tutu wanted to be a doctor but his family couldn't afford the training. He followed his father into teaching but was eventually ordained as an Anglican priest in 1961, inspired by Huddleston, and came the following year to study at King's College London and work as a part-time curate in Golders Green. He returned to South Africa in 1975 where he moved into his house on VilaKazi Street in Soweto, the street where Nelson Mandela used to live, and consequently one of the few streets in the world where two Nobel Prize winners have lived.

In the church he moved from being Dean of Johannesburg to Bishop of Lesotho, Bishop of Johannesburg and then Archbishop of Cape Town. This series of sermons asks us to look at saints for our times, those who have kept the rumour of God alive on the face of this earth. For me Tutu is high up there: a man whose faith has been courageous, outspoken, resilient, unapologetic but generous, liberating, attractive, who let his faith in Jesus Christ fire him up into both fight and fun so that the world really has been changed by it. So, briefly, why is he my inspiration today?

First, there is that faith. He has joked that when the English colonials arrived in Africa they had the Bible and the Africans had the land. The English said, 'Let us pray', and they closed their eyes and when they opened them the Africans had the Bible and the English had the land. The English like to say the sun never sets on their empire but that's only because God doesn't trust them in the dark! But Tutu, acknowledging gratefully much of what was brought to their shores educationally and so on, also says that it was a dangerous thing to do to give them the Bible. The Bible is a book about fighting oppression, about a God who isn't neutral but who is a biased God, biased in favour of the weak, the oppressed, the downtrodden and the despised. If you don't see that, he says, you are not reading the Bible but your own agenda.

His is a faith that believes that saints always have a past

and sinners always have a future, that a life of grace is always giving more than you owe and receiving more than you deserve. His faith is rooted in a biased, liberating, passionate God of mercy. And wherever he has been on his travels he always asks for some bread and wine to celebrate each day this God who is in communion with everyone, longing for their freedom. Once on a plane as he asked for the bread the helpful cabin crew asked if he'd like some butter with it. Well, you can't butter up God and ignore the truth that 'He took the side of the slaves, the victims. He is still the same even today, he sides with the poor, the hungry, the oppressed and victims of injustice.' You may be sitting in a garage but it doesn't make you a car. You may be sitting in a church but it doesn't make you a Christian if you fail to see that the God we worship can't help but step in on the side of those who are suffering and demands we do the same. We must stop gathering in the name of Jesus if we are ignoring the ways of Jesus.

Second, there is that courage. In 1976 the protests in Soweto against the government's use of Afrikaans as the compulsory language of instruction in black schools became an uprising against apartheid. From then on Tutu took a lead, supporting an economic boycott of his country, advocating non-violent protest, comparing apartheid to Nazism; consequently he had his passport revoked twice and was briefly jailed. When he brought his mother to London once they would stop a London policeman for directions even when they knew where they were going just, he says, for the novelty of having a police officer, a white police officer, speak to them courteously, addressing them as Sir or Madam.

His belief is strong: people are 'beautiful' because each is made in the image of God, and therefore to hate, imprison or discriminate is, as he calls it, spitting in the face of God. To degrade the dignity God places in every one of us is blasphemy. So where this happens the people of God must claim it back and free the injured. His bravery seemed to know no boundaries. 'I want the government to know,' he wrote, 'now and always that I do not fear them. They are trying to defend the utterly indefensible, and they will fail. They will fail because they are ranging themselves on the side of evil and injustice against the Church of God. Like others who have done that in the past – the Neros, the Hitlers, the Idi Amins of this world – they will end up as the flotsam and jetsam of history.' His heading up the Truth and Reconciliation Commission, based on the concept of restorative rather than retributive justice, was rooted in his belief in subsequent reconciliation being the work of God too.

Tutu remains controversial into our own day because of the comparisons he sees between apartheid and other injustices. He is outspoken about Israel/Palestine, climate change, China/Tibet, poverty, HIV/AIDS, cooperation among the world's faiths ('God is not a Christian', he reminds us), women's rights, family planning and assisted dying. He has taken a lead for LGBTQ people, saying: 'I would refuse to go to a homophobic heaven. No, I would say sorry, I mean I would much rather go to the other place. I would not worship a God who is homophobic and that is how deeply I feel about this. I am as passionate about this campaign as I ever was about apartheid. For me, it is at the same level.' You can imagine that many condemn him as being well on his way to the other place for saying this. But I, along with many others, remain profoundly grateful for his vision for those of us who are LGBTQ at this time in the Church. Like Jacob's ladder, it feels as if the messengers of God are in conversation with the earth. St Augustine said that 'Hope has two beautiful daughters: anger, at the ways things are, and courage, to put them right.'

Finally, there is his humour. I wanted to play a clip of Tutu laughing. It is so infectious, but all the clips are too long because once he starts he never stops. In one talk he tells a joke about Mary and Joseph getting to the stable. Joseph bangs on the door of the inn and asks: 'Please, please let us in, my wife is pregnant.' 'That's not my fault,' says the inn keeper. 'And it's not mine either,' says Joseph. Tutu then starts giggling, and then shrieking and belly-laughing with tears down his cheeks. I defy any of you not to join in. And that's it, I think: he wants us all to join in, and laughter helps. He wants us all to join in, be part of, church and society. It was he after all who coined the term 'the rainbow people of God'. He doesn't want some people to be tolerated. You tolerate haemorrhoids, you don't tolerate a child of God made in God's image, you reverence them and celebrate them, making sure you and they live together peaceably. If God is in communion with everyone so should we be, even if we must fight ideas and actions that work against this. As he says, my humanity is bound up with yours and we can only be human together.

So, when I grow up I want to be just a little bit like Desmond Tutu. To have just a little of his faith, his courage, his laughter and that contagious joy. In some ways we are seeing at the moment that when the Church lives in a cold climate, when people wonder what on earth we are for, the Church can get introverted and self-obsessed. Tutu teaches us that our faith is not just for us; it is to change lives. Our faith is not to save us from the world. It is for the world. This means being brave, even when you don't feel brave, and speaking honestly, passionately, truthfully. It often means being political when people tell you that you shouldn't be. It means understanding that Christian spirituality is about standing up for other people – seeing human beings as beautiful. And Tutu teaches us in all this not to take ourselves too seriously, not to let the cause of righteousness make us self-righteous but to laugh, surrender, lay down ourselves before God's mystery and know that no matter how big your head can get at times we are all very small and limited and wrong in the light of eternity. He once said to his close friend the Dalai Lama as they made their way to a press conference, 'The cameras are on us. For goodness' sake try to behave like a holy person.'

Nelson Mandela described Tutu as 'sometimes strident, often tender, never afraid and seldom without humour. His voice,' he said, 'will always be the voice of the voiceless.' And if that isn't a saint for our day then I don't know what is.

27

Is Life Beautiful?

For those who want to save their life will lose it,
and those who lose their life for my sake will find it.
Matthew 16.25

I tend to agree with Alfred Hitchcock that 'the length of a film should be directly related to the endurance of the human bladder'. However, one film that had a profound effect on me, long as it was, was *Schindler's List*, the Spielberg film of 1993 that focused on the unspeakable suffering at Auschwitz. I was not very happy, then, four years later to hear of another film, an Italian film, that also examined the suffering of the concentration camps but was funny in parts. It was called *Life is Beautiful*, and it was directed by Roberto Benigni, whose own father had been in such a camp. It won three Oscars and I was wrong to doubt it. I watch it again from time to time and sit, as usual, in tears at the end – it's then, of course, that someone calls round or telephones and thinks you're in a life crisis.

The first line of the film, spoken by the narrator, tells us: 'This is a simple story but not an easy one to tell.' The story is in two halves. The first is where we meet Guido, a Jewish waiter, funny, spontaneous, loving. He falls in love with Dora, a Catholic woman engaged to an unpleasant Fascist, and with touching relentless comic moments Guido woos her and eventually carries her off on a rainy night out of her restricting, class-ridden, unhappy life on his uncle's horse, which has been painted bright green by anti-Jewish thugs. In the midst of the threatening clouds of Fascism they celebrate together their pleasure in simple things: eggs, a bike, a kiss.

They marry and have a little son, Joshua, and to watch the three of them is an absolute joy. Guido makes everything fun. He loves Joshua with a reckless, spontaneous, deep love, and his wife with the same, and they all live as friends as well as family. It is, indeed, beautiful.

On Joshua's fourth birthday, though, Dora returns home to find that the Nazis have taken Guido and her son away to the train bound for the concentration camp. She races there and, although not a Jew, insists that the train is stopped so that she can get on it too. Although she is not in the same carriage, she is going with them. She cannot, will not, let them go on this journey without her.

At the camp, to survive the horror, Guido tells the little Joshua that they have entered a big game with lots of tests and that they have to score 1,000 points to win a brand-new real tank, by not complaining about being hungry, by hiding at certain points and doing what the game leaders in uniforms tell them to do. He pretends each day that he is going out to play hopscotch and 'ring a rosy' with the other men, while really he is burdened with carrying iron anvils that are slowly crushing his body. Guido hides the brutality by his fatherly fun. And when he stands to attention in the rain, shouted at and imprisoned by walls and dogs, he continues to smile for the sake of his son, just as he rescued Joshua's mum in the rain that day on a green horse.

Eventually the war looks as if it is ending and the soldiers are keen to cover up their evil deeds and get rid of the human evidence. There is panic and movement. Guido puts Joshua in a small postbox-shaped cupboard and tells him not to come out until everyone has gone because they are all looking for him because he is winning the game and if they find him he loses. Meanwhile in all the confusion Guido puts a scarf over his head and runs off to look for his wife. He is discovered by a searchlight, pinned on a wall. He is taken away and marched past the cupboard where his son is. They see one another through the postbox hole and Guido, true to the fun, to the game, to his love, winks and marches like a toy soldier to reassure his son that all's well and to make him smile one last time. We hear the bullets a few moments later.

Joshua is later rescued by US troops – in a tank! His dad was right, here is his prize! As he rides on the tank he sees his mother and calls out. They hug and hug, thin and tired, and Joshua shouts out: 'We won, Mama, we won! Here's the tank!' Joshua's voice then comes in, years later, as the film ends: 'This was the sacrifice my father made for me,' he says, 'it was his gift.'

In this series of sermons we are exploring the conversation there is often to be had between faith and film. *Life is Beautiful* has many lessons to enjoy in it, not least in the first half of watching a simple family survive in the midst of a prejudiced society, where sinister forces are at work but where they so clearly prove that happiness is not having what you want but wanting what you have. This is a film about the human spirit and its resilience. It is about life's possibilities, even in horror. It asks us what it might mean to lay aside your self in order to find it.

I was at a talk once when the speaker said that we should try and set aside an hour every day, a day every week and a week every year to stop striving: striving to have more and prove more. Instead we should stop in these times and see the gift and good we already have. Such sabbath times, he said, keep us human. Guido and his family celebrated the gift and good they had. Of course, political ideologies can remove this at whim, if given power. I was left wondering whether the question of what I would have done in the 1930s when Fascism was on the rise in Europe is best answered by asking myself what am I doing now when the same is happening in many places as I speak.

There are Christ figures in this film. Dora, though not a Jew, joins those on the way to their suffering. Her love cannot be separated from those who make up her life. She reflects God. Guido, similarly, works with contagious love and affection in the midst of evil to save the buoyancy of the human soul and spirit, to prove that hope and courage and humour and love are mightier than bullets and pain, mightier than a cross. 'Neither death, nor life, nor angels, nor rulers, nor things present, nor things to come,' says St Paul, 'will be able to separate us from God' – ever. In Guido's heart goodness is stronger than evil; love is stronger than hate; light is stronger than darkness; life is stronger than death. He does anything he can to protect and keep hope alive in his child. He reflects God. Joshua, which of course is the same name as Jesus, believes his father no matter what, and receives life because of it. 'This was the sacrifice my father made for me. It was his gift.' This is what Christians say of God.

A final thought: knowing that human beings like to identify a common enemy, usually an outsider, to keep their group together, an embodiment of evil on which they can throw their violence, we find Jesus asking his followers to break cycles of retributive hatred and to learn to touch the untouchable. Instead of the one being castigated by the 99, he tells a story of leaving the 99 to find the one. He dies as the unjustly persecuted scapegoat who willingly takes our violence on himself to break the circle and stop others being scapegoated, praying even as he dies for forgiveness not revenge. The cross is the judgement of judgement. He absorbs the hate as old as Cain's for Abel without passing it on and bids his followers do the same so that the mechanisms of projected hate are broken. He dies as we must live. In his own way Guido does the same. Robert Graves wrote a poem about Jesus alone in the desert for 40 days and nights and having only one friend with him, the little goat, the scapegoat that had also been sent out into the wilderness on the Day of Atonement, and under the stars of dark and lonely nights they kept themselves warm. There, against all the odds, life was beautiful.

28

A Gift to the World

Love never ends.
1 Corinthians 13.8

There was a story in the news some years ago about an Englishman called Eric King-Turner, aged 102, who set sail to go and live in New Zealand to, in his words, 'start a new life'. He was Britain's oldest emigrant. And why? Because Doris, his wife, originally from New Zealand, was feeling homesick and they felt that they should make the move. Love obviously kept them young. It reminded me of a pensioner in my first parish who, tapping at his grey hair one day, said to me: 'Just because there's snow on the roof doesn't mean the fire has gone out!'

Well, today is St Valentine's Day. We don't know much about St Valentine except that he was one of several early martyrs killed in Rome for their Christian faith and that he was buried on the Via Flaminia, north of the city, on 14 February. It wasn't until 496 that the Pope named a day in his memory and even then he didn't tell us much more about him. Some old traditions, however, say that he was a priest or a bishop, and by 1260 one of the most-read books of the High Middle Ages, the *Golden Legend*, says that Emperor Claudius had commanded Valentine in the year 280 to deny Christ before him. Valentine refused and so Claudius had him beheaded, but before this happened Valentine restored the sight of his jailer's daughter. Later additions to this story say that it was when the daughter opened a letter from Valentine that her sight came back and she was able to read 'from your Valentine' written at the bottom. Children loved Valentine

A GIFT TO THE WORLD

very much and missed him while he was in prison and pushed flowers through the bars of his window to cheer him up.

Another tradition says that the Emperor was finding it difficult to get men to sign up to the army because nobody wanted to leave their wives and so he banned engagements and weddings. The priest Valentine defied this by secretly marrying people. When he was discovered he was murdered.

The fourteenth-century writer Geoffrey Chaucer based one of his works on the popular belief that around the feast of Valentine the birds choose their mates. Happily, churches celebrate many birds who have chosen their mates by giving them the opportunity to exchange solemn vows before the altar in marriage. And Christians believe that as such vows are spoken something of God is unveiled.

In Jeremiah, God says: 'All your lovers have forgotten you; they care nothing for you' (30.14). Now, this is how you may have felt this morning if you didn't get a Valentine's card; but often in the Scriptures the relationship between God and his people is described in terms of a marriage or a loving relationship, and when we wander off and seek our thrills and boosts elsewhere God laments it as if we were unfaithful to him. All through the Bible we see men and women trying to live with God learning how to be faithful in this relationship called faith, having to get over the romance of belief (the highs and unrealism) and settle into a way of being together with him that is stable, sometimes pedestrian, but the deepest strength of your everyday, a relationship in which more is communicated in silence together, a way of growing into trust.

The vows of a marriage are one of the Church's gifts to the world.

I take you, to have and to hold from this day forward

That is, I won't grip and I won't let go. I'll have you in my life and I'll hold you with care.

For better, for worse,

So, whatever comes our way. We don't know how life will go but we'll be there together.

For richer, for poorer,

Money helps in this life but it isn't who we are and we'll still love each other even if we lose everything.

In sickness and in health,

I'll be there when you need me; even if it means me giving up my freedom, I'll be there.

To love and to cherish,

I won't manage it, but I will try to freshen my love for you every day.

Till death us do part.

I don't want to think about it, but it will happen. I'll always know you were mine and I was yours and that memory will keep me going.

All that I am I give to you,
All that I have I share with you.

What more can one human being say to another?

This is love, not romance, and it is practical, brave, patient, sacrificial. God's fidelity to us is reflected in such promises and also, I believe, in the lives of faithfully loving people who are not always able or permitted to make such promises in church. All that God is God shares with us.

And those who travel through life without a partner, who do not feel drawn to partnership or who for whatever reason have not met the right person, often learn to love in similar ways, loving people, perhaps friends and family, in committed and sacrificial ways. I have always disliked the term 'family service' because every service is the place where we all, whether single, partnered, divorced or bereaved, come together and make up the family we are as a church. And it is the place where we all come to learn the lessons of love that Christ teaches.

And if you want to do a quick check as to how well you are doing learning the lessons of love, here's a way. You will know that a popular reading at weddings is 1 Corinthians 13 when Paul tells us what love is – patient, kind, never boastful nor rude. The way to check how you are doing as a Christian is to place I in the reading instead of love: 'I am patient, I am kind, I envy no one, I am never rude, I am never puffed up or arrogant. I never insist on my own way, never rejoice in wrongdoing, never irritable, never resentful.' Hmmm ... as someone once said, it took God seven days to make heaven and earth but he's still working on me!

The love that Valentine showed was not romantic but a love with willpower and courage. Lives changed and ended because of it. If we could reclaim Valentine's love, taking it away from cooing doves and podgy cherubs on cards, and bringing it down to earth as the letter of St Paul does and as the marriage vows do too, then we would know why it is important to celebrate his memory and to recall that all human love, no matter in whom, or where or when it finds its life and stability, is a small, limited but beautiful reflection of God's giving of himself to us that needs to be cherished for the gift it is.

29

Alone in Berlin

'Zacchaeus, hurry and come down'
Luke 19.5

This week I went to see Vincent Perez's film *Alone in Berlin*. It is based on a novel written in 1947 by Hans Fallada called *Every Man Dies Alone*. And I will, if I may, just briefly outline the story.

It's 1940 in Berlin and a working-class couple, Otto and Anna Quangel, receive news that their only son has been killed in action. At the same time, an elderly Jewish woman neighbour of theirs is suffering lawless behaviour against her which results in her throwing herself to her death from a window. Impelled by these events, the couple start writing postcards to urge people to stand against Hitler and the Nazis and they furtively place these cards in public places, mainly apartment blocks where ordinary people come across them as they come home. Although their marriage at first appears to have dried up, being unable to console each other for the loss of their son, their shared risk and commitment to resistance, writing and delivering the cards brings them back to one another, in effect falling in love with each other all over again.

The police inspector charged with finding the source of these postcards has professional pride but is no convinced Nazi, and over three years spent trying to trace the culprits he develops a sort of respect for whoever is doing this.

One day some of the cards accidentally fall out of Otto's pocket while at work and he is arrested. He tries in vain to convince the police that it was only him writing the cards and not his wife but they both end up in court, briefly managing to hold hands and telling each other that they know their fate and it doesn't matter. They know that the love, so bereaved in their son's loss, has done all that it could do and that is enough for them now. As Otto is led to his cell the officer asks if he can get him anything. 'A card and a pen,' he replies. Otto and Anna are both executed.

Back at the station, the police officer gathers up all the subversive cards he has collected over the years, nearly 300 of them, and scatters them out of the window into the street for all to read, before shooting himself. As the cards swirl in the wind you feel Otto and Anna have a moral victory beyond the grave. At the end of the film a tribute appears on the screen, dedicating the film to Otto and Elise Hampel, the two real people in wartime Berlin on whom the story is based. They left cards in stairwells and apartment blocks all over the city and, a stark reminder of the brutality of those days, were both beheaded for it.

Let's change gear and move to another story but maybe not so different, that of Zacchaeus. His name means 'righteous' but no one would have chosen a word like that to describe him. He belonged to a despised group of Jewish citizens who were employed by the Romans to collect taxes from their own people and who were notorious for extortion, greed and deceit. He was, we are told, a chief tax collector, one who employed tax collectors under him to collect revenues throughout his district. We are told he was rich. I bet he was. But not respected. That's why people grumbled when Jesus calls Zacchaeus down from the tree, and goes into his home. And we don't really know what happened then but Jesus, I suspect, did what Jesus did – he engaged Zacchaeus with stories, parables even, conversation that brought about some receptive insight. He will have listened to Zacchaeus and he will have read between the man's lines and seen his need, his longing, his hunger for a different life. He will have seen where his heart had grown cold. Whatever was said that day, it had amazing results. Zacchaeus decides to give away half of what he possesses and to pay back four times the amount he has cheated people out of. And Jesus says that 'salvation' – healing and integrity – has come to his house.

Otto and Elise Hampel took simple messages into people's homes to subvert the powers of the day that were insisting on obedience and fear. They, in their simple way, sought to undermine tyranny and call people back to their humanity, to reacquaint themselves with their values and their willpower to stand against evil. Jesus did the same. He took his vision of the kingdom of God into homes and human hearts in order to subvert the rules we so unthinkingly and ordinarily live by. Lives that simmer us down, take away the dignity and liberty of the children of God we all are. When the Hampels took their cards into the housing blocks they, in their simple but brave way, were reflecting something of the Christ who challenges the world's darker behaviours to reclaim God's better path to peace.

The story of Zacchaeus is an invitation to become a new person, defined in a new way, to trade in all the words that have described him up to now – rich, respected, cultured, educated, obedient to the corrupt and powerful system – to trade these in for one radically different word, which is 'free'. Zacchaeus was, it seems, possessed by what he possessed, trapped by his trappings, and, if it wasn't just trees he climbed but social and influential ladders, then he met a man who taught him it was time to come down and live. The great mythologist Joseph Campbell said that most of us reach a point in life when, having spent so much time and energy in life trying to climb up on to the roof, we discover when we get there that it's the wrong house and we must start again, this time being accountable to our ideals and values rather than just to our interests. St Augustine similarly prays in his *Confessions*: 'Grant, Lord, that I may know myself that I may know thee.'

Like Zacchaeus we all have a little time left on this earth, and the gospel's grace, like a small message of reality brought into your home, into your heart, gives us time for amendment in life to make sure we're living and not just self-justifying or competing. Zacchaeus ended that day with much less of what he had thought was important to being a successful man but with much more of what he knew was vital to being a human being, fully alive in love and God. He was poorer that day but free. Now it's our turn.

30

Have You a Mind to Sink?

'Unless these men stay in the ship, you cannot be saved.'
Acts 27.31

Having once been the Rector of the 'Actors' Church' in
Covent Garden, theatre has always been an important part
of my life and its urgent search for wisdom. I have seen some
amazing productions over the years but I wonder if any of
them were as startling as that of *The Tempest* directed by
Chris Goode at the Edinburgh Festival in 2000.

Many of you will know that *The Tempest* begins with
a storm and a shipwreck and takes us to an island – often
in literature and myth a place of human testing, a place of
magical but dangerous dislocation of the soul. Shakespeare's
short play is notoriously ambiguous, charged with a blend
of magic, music, humour, intrigue and tenderness, that has
over the centuries been read in so many different ways, from
a romance of reconciliation to a Christian allegory of forgiveness, from a meditation on the powers of imagination and
the limits of art to a psychological drama of fatherhood,
from a play about Jacobean politics to a dramatization of
colonialist or patriarchal ideology. This indeterminacy is, it
can be argued, written into the narrative and leads to the
often-quoted comment of Anne Barton: '*The Tempest* is an
extraordinarily obliging work of art. It will lend itself to
almost any interpretation, any set of meanings imposed upon
it: it will even make them shine.'

Even the characters baffle. Is Prospero admirable or detest-
able? Is Caliban bestial or noble? Is Ariel loyal or resentful?
Is Miranda demure or resilient? This elusiveness can lead to a

tempest inside, a sense of being rocked about and struggling to keep your head above the waters of understanding, or its mysteriousness could be its beauty and strength, maybe a mature play asking us to be at ease with ambiguities, not least our own: a play that not so much cannot be talked about with certainty so much as one that can be endlessly talked about with adventure. It all depends, in words from the first scene, on the question: 'Have you a mind to sink?'

The production in Edinburgh was performed in local people's houses and flats. You offered your home and the six actors turned up like strolling players and began the play without any fuss. It took place in semi-darkness with improvised lighting from torches, bicycle lamps, candles and fairy lights. At the end the actors evaporated into the night like shy spirits without even taking a bow. It was a stark reminder that theatre is an experience you have, not a place that you go to.

Chris Goode believed that people's homes are simply the best place to perform a play that is all about changing perceptions, altered states and geographical confusions, allowing him and the cast to take the audience on a journey in which the familiar became disconcertingly unfamiliar. So in an Edinburgh flat, a bedroom doorway became Caliban's lair and Ferdinand was found undertaking Prospero's tasks – better known as washing up in the kitchen. Miranda and Prospero's murmured conversation heard just a foot away was Shakespeare spoken in your living room, not declaimed on a stage. It was if you were eavesdropping. At the end, in pitch black, stunned for a few seconds, the audience came to as if they were awaking from a dream – to find the actors gone. At every performance, somewhere in your home the actors had left behind a small paper boat, on the mantelpiece or by the bed, or resting by the window. A small reminder that it hadn't all been a dream; it had happened and under your own roof.

Early Christians spoke of Jesus as Word, walking into the land of our homes, visiting us for a short time and in that time subverting us, our priorities and selfish comforts, our so-called 'common' sense and deep and destructive prejudices. He was making the familiar strange again. In that short time, repicturing God for us, redefining the boundaries of love – if there are such things. This man walks in and creates a storm of the human spirit, blasting complacency where it has become oppressive and creating a calm where struggling lives need assurance and peace. In many ways this life in our earth-home was a tempest of changing perceptions, altered states and talk of a kingdom far off that feels like our desired harbour. He brought an energy, a hope, a new way of being that defrosted the heart: if only you had the ears to hear, he said, if only you could tune in, tune in your lives to this brave new world of God.

A few years later in that story we find not a small paper boat but a small wooden one, on choppy seas with Paul and some friends, a boat with early disciples of Jesus carrying his message to other places, other homes. It had not been a magical illusion for them: it was reality, and their boats set out with the precious treasure of their witness with similar danger to refugees in our own time. It was risky but it was a message that could save us from ourselves, so they set off. For them, like theatre, church was not a place to go, there weren't any built yet. Church was an experience of change, a way of translating the life and holy storm of this man into ordinary day-to-day life and relationships, not alone but together; with baptism forging a sort of new family, water was now thicker than blood. Peter, a stormy man himself in many ways, preached again and again that this Jesus story hadn't ended, though, he hadn't come and gone and left us in the dark, but in fact, the Jesus movement had only just begun and now was to be continued – continued in you – if you think it's important enough, that is. The paper boat is left on your mantelpiece. Is it all just a dream? Or do you have the ears to hear, spoken to you as close as it gets: 'Follow me.'

31

Breivik

Whoever does not love does not know God,
for God is love.
1 John 4.8

On 22 July 2011 I felt very sick. I was watching TV and the events that unfolded in Norway at a summer camp. It was the day Anders Behring Breivik murdered 77 people in cold blood, running after innocent people, disguised as a policeman, hunting them down. He shot 69 people, the youngest 14 years old, after planting a bomb in the capital, Oslo, that had murdered another eight people. At his trial, in his long manifesto he made it clear that he was engaged in a crusade to re-Christianize Europe. He is, he claimed, a baptized Christian and he acted so the truth could be seen that only the cross of Christian faith will unify the people of Europe. Muslims and left-liberals need to be expelled or exterminated.

To hear the faith to which I have tried to commit my life, my thinking, my actions, spoken of in the way Breivik did in those ensuing days made me sick to the core. It bore no resemblance at all, indeed was the very demonic opposite, to the God I see in Jesus Christ and in the way of love he preached and lived. How could my faith be so politically perverted? How could it be so confident and yet so far from what the majority believe who call themselves Christian? How could a faith of sacrificial love have been soured into a regime of sacrificing murder?

Many Muslims are watching their TVs at the moment and feeling the same. And when they leave their homes and walk in the street many walk in fear of being attacked in some coarse act of revenge. Members of the Jewish community, too, have increasing fear, and schools and synagogues are being tensely guarded. Christians in many parts of the world are living in fear of their lives. And the secular extremists, the secular commentators shout 'a plague on all their houses'. The world would be better off without religion if this is what it does. And there are days when even the most devout give a passing thought to whether they might be right.

And yet. I remind myself again that what is being perpetrated in the name of religion is not true to those religions. We cannot stop criminals using God as some sort of back-up to their hate crimes, but we can continue to say, no, that is not the God that Christianity, Islam and Judaism worship. And we must bring people of those faiths together to show this to each other as well as to those who would wish they'd all somehow disappear so the world could be God-less – as if that would somehow make it more peaceful or just. Faiths will need to remind the democratic world that while to be democratic you occasionally need a bit of incivility carefully applied – we all need scrutiny – you also need a lot of civility liberally applied for the common good to flourish. Liberty, yes. Equality, yes. But we also, remember, need fraternity, and that needs thinking through carefully.

Then there is the question of God caught up in all this politics: another victim alongside those murdered. Times like this make me search as to why I continue to pursue this God when so many who say they act in his name are creating a religion of death not life. And time and time again I go back to some words spoken by the writer Dennis Potter as his life drew to an end with cancer. In an interview with Melvyn Bragg broadcast on Channel 4 in April 1994, he was asked, weak as he was, whether he had now thrown God off? He replied:

Religion has always been – I've said it before, it doesn't matter that I repeat myself, I won't get many more chances to repeat myself, thank God – but religion has always been the wound and not the bandage. I don't see the point of not acknowledging the pain and the misery and the grief of the world, and if you say 'Ah, but God understands' or 'through that you come to a greater appreciation' ... I mean, I don't think, well you nasty old sod, if that's God ... that's not God, that's not my God, that's not how I see God. I see God in us or with us, if I see at all, as some shreds, particles, rumours, some knowledge that we have, some feeling why we sing and dance and act, why we paint, why we love, why we make art. All the things that separate us from the purely animal in us are palpably there, and you can call them what you like, and you can theologize about them, and you can build great structures of belief about them. The fact is – they are there and I have no means of knowing whether that thereness in some sense doesn't cling to what I call me.

I find these words very powerful. Potter was an irritant all his life to the Establishment and the conventional, and as much of an irritant to the unthinking or lazy, challenging any agnosticism as well as any orthodoxy. And here, I believe, he pinpoints something very important, namely that belief in God comes out of an intuition, a sense of awe, epiphany, surprise, beyond-ness; out of a perception that reality can somehow ultimately be trusted, a sense that love and life have a source and a goal. And though loud, aggressive voices take us away from these whispers within, to return to them can be a source of peace, for us and those around us. You discover that God is as close as a spouse to us, that all human beings are temples of God, and that we meet God in each other.

It is a strange world where we have to search for God in the very opposite of what those who say they know God best will tell us. But as Christians we follow a man who was opposed from the start to religious cruelty and who lived a life he now invites us to live with him that speaks and acts in one truth: 'where charity and love are, there is God'. There and nowhere else.

32

Hypocrisy

'Beware of the yeast of the Pharisees,
that is, their hypocrisy.'
Luke 12.1

In the south-west tower of St Paul's Cathedral some years ago there was an unusual installation by the architect John Pawson. Sitting on a reflective hemisphere at the bottom of the Geometric Stair was a large concave crystal, and high above it, at the top of the stair's chamber, a convex mirror. Pawson invited us to look into the crystal to see the complex combination of light, space and proportion of the staircase above in a fresh and startling way. You had to watch at which angle you came towards the crystal, though, or you got a rather frightening close-up of your own face, looking haggard and surprised and sporting an unstylish number of chins.

In many ways, the teaching of Jesus found in Luke's Gospel has spiritual comparisons to this, as he asks us to look within to see what is being reflected. Jesus is fierce with the devout leaders and biblical interpreters of the day, the lawyers. And he summarized his teaching one day like this: 'Beware of the yeast of the Pharisees, that is, their hypocrisy.' Beware of hypocrisy.

As a priest, one gets a lot of people tell you at dinner parties or at the bus stop why they don't believe in God or go to church. One complaint you hear time and time again is that Christians are a bunch of hypocrites: they talk about love and confess their sins and say they are saved and others aren't, then they go and live just as they want to. So stories such as that of Ted Haggard, the pastor in Colorado Springs, adviser to the powerful and President of the National Evangelical Association which represents 30 million American Christians, who was well known for his robust and unrelenting attacks on homosexuality and drugs and who was later exposed as having a class-A drug-infused relationship with a male prostitute, well, such stories fuel the charge of Christian hypocrisy. When Jimmy Swaggart, another millionaire moralistic preacher, was similarly found consorting with prostitutes he memorably told his congregation following the revelations that the Lord had told him that it was none of their business.

Now it is strange, if not tragic, that one of the charges against Christians is hypocrisy when one of the things we know about Jesus is that he hated hypocrisy. He couldn't stand it, and got angry when talking about it. He confronts it with quite a force. 'This people honours me with their lips but their hearts are far from me.' The lesson: God hates hypocrisy, that state of pretending to be someone, to believe things, to do things, that are just not true to who you are or are even in opposition to the facts. Hypocrisy is a performance and involves the deception of others and is thus a kind of lie; eventually the lie becomes your life and you spiritually drain away. A hypocrite lies with sincerity and often stops seeing the deception. The mask begins to eat into the face.

Nathaniel Hawthorne once noted that: 'No one for any considerable period can wear one face to himself and another to the multitude without finally getting bewildered as to which may be the true.'

The former Bishop of Oxford tells the story of when he was a vicar and went to take an assembly in his local school wearing his cassock. A girl asked him, 'Mr Pritchard, are you pretending to be a vicar?' He says this question has haunted him ever since.

There is a difference between preaching ideals and being honest as to how you find it hard to live up to them yourself, and being deceptive about the distance between what you say and what you do, although they can sometimes feel similar. Let me tell you, preaching about hypocrisy instantly makes you feel a hypocrite. The Greek philosopher Aristotle thought a lot about friendship and he concluded that true friendship is not a perfect relationship. Rather, true friendship is the environment in which we learn how to be friends. True friendship is not some ideal that actual friendships never achieve but is a growing relationship that as it increases transforms ourselves and our friendship. Whereas Christians pursue ideals, and even preach ideals, we always need to discover ways in which to practise our Christian faith in a way that allows us to make mistakes and learn from them. It is not the hypocrite who falls short of the mark – that is the sinner. The hypocrite, the actor or pretender, is the one who is so arrogant and complacent that he doesn't know or doesn't care that he falls short. That's why Jesus shouts at them to stop their snoring through life and wake up to themselves.

Hypocrisy is a failure of conscience, a spiritual blind spot, a lack of self-awareness. Faith, like friendship, is true as long as it is being worked at, is being constantly learned. The discipline we need as Christians is to work each day, in each situation and each encounter, for a bit more honesty: in and about ourselves, what we are thinking, feeling, believing, who we are before God and each other. Like the Pawson installation, this will need a peering within to see how our past is reflecting itself through us and to see how we are to live the rest of our life – either as a prisoner to our pretences and public performances or as a disciple of Christ able to live with the joy of being wrong.

The funeral in 2011 of Otto von Habsburg, the last heir to the Austro-Hungarian empire, took place in Vienna. In the tradition of Habsburg funerals when his body arrived at the Capuchin church to be interred the doors were found shut. The herald knocked on the door. A monk from behind the doors asked: 'Who demands entry?' The herald read out the titles of the deceased: 'Otto of Austria; former Crown Prince of Austria-Hungary; Prince Royal of Hungary and Bohemia, of Dalmatia, Croatia, Slavonia, Galicia, Lodomeria, and Illyria; Grand Duke of Tuscany and Cracow; Duke of Lorraine, of Salzburg, Styria, Carinthia, Carniola and Bukowina; Grand Prince of Siebenbürgen, Margrave of Moravia; Duke of Silesia, Modena, Parma, Piacenza, Guastalla, Auschwitz and Zator, Teschen, Friuli, Dubrovnik and Zadar; Princely Count of Habsburg and Tyrol, of Kyburg, Gorizia and Gradisca; Prince of Trent and Brixen and so on.' At the end the monk said: 'We know him not.' The herald knocked again: 'Who demands entry?' came the voice. 'Dr Otto von Habsburg.' 'We know him not.' A third knock. 'Who demands entry?' 'A sinner in need of God's mercy.' 'Him we know,' said the monk, and the doors were opened.

The doors of grace do indeed open when we confront who we really are without fear, without illusions, and with trust that with God's help I shall become myself. What will stop us? 'Beware the yeast of the Pharisees, that is, their hypocrisy.'

33

Caesar and Scottsboro

'Give to the emperor the things that are the emperor's,
and to God the things that are God's.'
Mark 12.17

OK. I think it's time I came out. I've been hiding for too long, hoping nobody would guess, but it's time to admit it. I love musicals. It's not cool but I can't help it. I know they can cheapen theatrical experience, I know hum-ability is not the pinnacle of musical quality, I know the stories can be ridiculous – but I love musicals. There, I've said it. I feel better already. Now you might even be able to tell what brand of Christian I am from my favourite musical. If I'm evangelical, it might well be *The King and I*. A Puritan? It has to be *Ain't Misbehavin*. A Liberal? *Anything Goes*. A tele-evangelist will want *Jesus Christ Superstar*. And if I keep this up and preach too long you'll be *Les Misérables*. So, where's this all going?

Well, a musical opened in London in 2013 called *The Scottsboro Boys*. It tells the true story of nine black teen-agers accused of raping two women in Alabama in 1931. All but the 13-year-old were sentenced to death by electro-cution in a hasty trial with poor legal representation and an all-white jury, who could hear a lynch mob outside the court demanding that the accused be handed over to them. After a series of appeals and retrials over six years, and one of the two women admitting that she had made up the rape story, charges were finally dropped for four of the nine defendants. Sentences for the rest ranged from 75 years to death. All but two served prison sentences. One was shot in prison by a guard. Some of the men's convictions were overturned; one defendant, Clarence Norris, received a pardon in 1976. At his death in 1989, he was the only Scottsboro boy known to be alive. Others in later life had disappeared, maybe using other names to protect themselves from lynch mobs. It was only in 2013 that Alabama's parole board voted to grant posthumous pardons to the Scottsboro boys, recognizing a grave miscarriage of justice. As officials said: 'This decision will give them a final peace in their graves, wherever they are. They have finally received justice.'

A question: looking back, what do you hope the Church said and did during those trials and after them? Should Christian leaders and congregations have got involved at all or should they have left it to the state, to the officers of Caesar?

We think today about the role of the Church in society. And three models are often promoted. The first sees faith in the realm of the purely personal. Faith is about inwardness and feeling. So if society is inhumane and objective, faith is the guardian of the human and the subjective. Faith here is about personal and free decisions, not about social behaviour, political responsibility or economic action. Faith is about inner unburdening and personal readjustment, so questions about social reality rarely get priority.

The second model is faith as fellowship, faith as providing not just community but co-humanity. Loneliness and isolation are the enemies and a congregation sets out here to provide what might be lacking in society – warmth, acceptance, authenticity. Faith provides an alternative, a counterbalance to society. Find your true home here, not there.

The third model is faith as institution, institutionalizing faith for balance and order amid society's rapid changes. Confidence in the institution's authority is promoted so that people become less accountable for their own decisions. One doesn't need to understand so much as accept. Institutions tend to be cautious and compromised as they engage with authorities, and those attracted to institutions quickly begin to reflect them.

Three models of faith that we can easily recognize today – but which would have helped the Scottsboro boys? A Church of personal purity, a Church asking you to step out of the world into its own welcome, or an institution led by those seeking approval from the majority, the judiciary, the government? The answer, of course, is that all could help and have done so in history but too often these models have failed by having little to say to society other than what society wants to hear – that religion and politics shouldn't really mix.

There is a fourth model and it was embodied by people such Martin Luther King Jr. 'The early Christians,' he said, 'rejoiced when they were deemed worthy to suffer for what they believed. In those days the Church was not merely a thermometer that recorded the ideas and principles of popular opinion; it was a thermostat that transformed the mores of society.'

In this model the Church still offers personal transformation, a fellowship of co-humanity and even order and continuity through its organization, but first of all it is pioneering for the kingdom of God. It seeks to embody hope for the world by challenging what is unjust, unfair and sometimes un-nameable because God has a dream of a different way of being a world that we have signed up to. Isn't that why we're here now? King's dream was God's dream but to make it come about the Church first had to wake up. This will not be a Church out of the world but a Church for the world. But to be that there will often be a cost – of ridicule, or being sidelined, or losing members, or being told to get back to our proper business of floral and choral entertainment for the religiously inclined. But Christians only have one person to imitate – who also bore the cost. 'I have tried to make it clear that it is wrong to use immoral means to attain moral ends,' said King. 'But now I must affirm that it is just as wrong, or even more so, to use moral means to preserve immoral ends.' He preached: 'We know through painful experience that freedom is never voluntarily given by the oppressor; it must be demanded by the oppressed.' And when they have no voice, we must do it for them. That's embodying hope: a Church with a spirituality of speaking for others. This is giving God what is God's and letting Caesar know about it.

Jesus took a bit of metal and asked whose image was stamped on it. Fine. Give it back to him. But he spent his ministry holding human beings and asking the same question. Whose image is stamped here? And the answer? God's. So look after this, then. Don't you dare throw this down or think you can buy and spend it like a coin. Cherish. Bring hope. Restore the dignity of that lovingly impressed, sealed with the image of God. And that's why two clergy, the Episcopalian George McDowell and the Presbyterian Henry Edmonds, worked hard despite the fury of the crowds to get justice for the Scottsboro boys in the name of the Lord who also suffered murderous injustice. And it is why we now, in our day, have a duty to speak and act when and wherever decisions are made, be it society, governments home or abroad, churches, workplace or home, that do not uphold that image of God in each and every human person: diminishing them by low pay, taking away their voice or rights, fantasizing a worldview that conveniently forgets those who don't fit theories. No. Look after the things that are God's and Caesar might eventually take notice. King sets us our challenge now. He wrote while in prison in Birmingham in April 1963:

I am coming to feel that the people of ill will have used time much more effectively than the people of goodwill. We will have to repent in this generation not merely for the vitriolic words and actions of the bad people, but for the appalling silence of the good people. We must come to see that human progress never rolls in on wheels of inevitability. It comes through the tireless efforts and persistent work of men and women willing to be co-workers with God, and without this hard work time itself becomes an ally of the forces of social stagnation. We must use time creatively, and forever realize that the time is always ripe to do right.

So give to Caesar the fuss he needs but remind him continually, relentlessly, courageously, who has our first loyalty.

34

Submissive or Subversive?

'Blessed are you among women'
Luke 1.42

Not too long ago I went to see a friend I've known for 15 years in hospital. We talked, smiled, swapped news and then I said goodbye, telling him when I would next visit. The following night at a quarter to midnight I was standing in the same hospital room next to his lifeless body, now saying prayers of commendation for the peace of his soul. I was struck, as I often am, at how Robert's body did indeed look peaceful. We had been laughing the day before. He had told me the story about Oscar Wilde dying in a hotel room and how he hated the wallpaper and had complained about it for ages. Eventually as he lay dying he said to a friend, looking at the wallpaper again, 'Well, one of us had to go.' Robert had felt the same about the hospital room. But when I went into it again, though cancer had done its worst there appeared on that human face, in the faceless room, a still, individual dignity that would never be seen again on this earth. Although the spirit was no longer in the body, the animation taken away, he appeared to sleep.

The idea of death as a sleeping is found in the Scriptures from time to time. The Greek word for sleeping, *koimesis*, is the root of our word cemetery, which literally means 'a place of sleep'. And in the Eastern Orthodox Churches, 15 August is known as the Koimesis of Mary, often translated into English as the Dormition of Mary, her 'falling asleep'. Orthodox icons often portray the dormition of Mary. Traditionally, she is lying on a bed surrounded by the apostles, and up above you see Jesus holding in his arms what appears to be a baby in swaddling clothes. This is the childlike soul of his mother which he embraces and cherishes, just as she had held him in her arms at his birth and at his death. In Western art, this scene became less common and eventually disappeared, although Caravaggio, in typical provocative manner, in 1606 painted his *Death of the Virgin* in which Mary, an obviously frail human form with swollen feet and lifeless arms, dies in such an inglorious way that it was rejected by the church it was commissioned for as unfit for devotion.

What the devout found more acceptable were those portraits of Mary such as you find beautifying the Sainsbury Wing of the National Gallery, in which she is taken up to heaven, body and soul: 'assumed' into heaven. So 15 August is also known as the Assumption of Mary. Here she is crowned as the Queen of Heaven by her Son as all the saints and angels look on. Although this story is not found in the Bible it was a very early Christian belief that Mary enjoyed the faithful promises of her Son: 'If I go and prepare a place for you, I will come again, and will receive you to myself; that where I am, you may be there also.' She is an example of one who trusted Christ and an obvious model for all those who try to follow him. As she believed in him in her life, so she participated in resurrection at her death. Debates were had as to whether it was just her soul, or her body and soul, that was taken to heaven. For those who believed the latter there was the legend that when Mary lay dying all the apostles travelled to be with her. St Thomas was three days late, and didn't believe, as was his wont, that she had been assumed. So the legend has it that she dropped down her girdle to him to prove it. You will see this in many medieval pictures: Thomas catching the red rope as it falls.

Now Roman Catholics and Anglicans sometimes struggle to believe the same things, but fairly recently an agreed long statement was written about Mary, because over history she has been the source of so much disagreement and division. You will know the objections to Marian devotion: that she gets in the way of Christ, that statues of her are idolatrous, that the images of her as a submissive girl are demeaning to women and a product of patriarchal stereotyping, that the miracles attested to her seem phoney and that visions of her are results of individual or group psychosis. As one sceptic said, 'The assumption is the most aptly named dogma of all.'

In answer to this, those who reverence Mary do so as an encouragement to their faith: here was one who suffered and trusted and fulfilled the Christian life. She gives us hope. She also brings a necessary feminine element into Christian theology. That was why Jung was so interested in the Assumption, because he believed it celebrated the feminine within the Godhead that so often gets pushed out by our male church hierarchies and God-talk.

Well, what the Roman Catholic and Anglican statement agreed was this: that it is impossible to be faithful to the Bible and not to give due attention to Mary. And it was acknowledged that Mary was prepared by grace to be the mother of our Redeemer, by whom she herself was redeemed and received into glory, and that we recognize Mary as a model of holiness, faith and obedience for all Christians. And so both the Roman Catholic Church and the Anglican Church, as well as the Orthodox churches, keep 15 August in her honour. As she says in the Gospel: 'All generations shall call me blessed.' As the Bible recalls, the angel addressed her: 'Hail Mary, full of grace. The Lord is with you.' And she was also told: 'Blessed are you among women and blessed is the fruit of your womb.' For many Christians, to pray the words of the angel and say 'Hail Mary' is simply to call to mind and to heart a Christian friend in whom we see the fullness of all that Christ came to bring.

A final thought about Mary: Mary's song at the beginning of Luke's Gospel is said or sung every evening in the Church's evening services. It's considered to be that important – the problem being, of course, that the beautiful musical settings it has been given, or even the language itself, can distract us from the actual ideas contained in the song. The ironies are not lost on me as I sit in my high-up wooden stall as Mary sings: 'He has put down the mighty from their seats and exalted the humble.' I wonder sometimes what other ironies we might be missing.

The song is known as the Magnificat, the first word of the Latin translation of Mary's hymn: 'My soul magnifies the Lord'. Magnify isn't a word we use much except when we describe what a magnifying glass does. It enlarges. This is what Mary is doing when she starts singing. She wants to draw attention to the greatness of God.

Mary's Magnificat, however, is no sentimental hymn. Biblical scholars often call it revolutionary, upturning the standards of the contemporary world. If the Church always needs the 'leaven of discontent' then we have it here, a continual reminder of the priorities of God and his first love, of the poor and forgotten. The truth of Mary's song is that while we have tried to make her a submissive woman we have failed to see she was a subversive one. She teaches us here that the way to know if God is being born in the messy stable of your life is if God revolutionizes the way you think, the way you act and the way you treat other people. The ego, the rich, the proud, the mighty – they must be resisted as the influences and priorities of a human life. They must be put down from their seats. The hungry, the poor, the oppressed, the weak – these instead lie in the heart of God's compassion, and Christian spirituality means to stand with them. These are the exalted.

It is always possible to be part of a land and not be part of the revolution, even to go to the revolution's festivities and not be part of the revolution. By singing or saying the Magnificat every day of the year at Evening Prayer the

Church is reminding the worshipper that it is possible to be part of the congregation and not be part of God's revolution. The Magnificat places a compass in the heart of the evening service to point us back to the heart of God. This woman who sang of divine liberation for oppressed peoples is not made of plaster or plastic. She is very much alive and is still singing out for all who are unloved and overlooked. Will we join in?

35

The Unnamed Man

'There was a rich man who was dressed in purple'
Luke 16.19

If you go into a bookshop at the moment, and manage to get past all the 'how to get rich quick' books which unnervingly nestle next to shelves of books on 'how to raise your low self-esteem', you will find a novel by Mitch Albom. It's called *The Five People You Meet in Heaven,* and without telling you too much, it's a moving story about an old man called Eddie who dies and goes to heaven. When he's there, he discovers that everybody in heaven has to meet five people, and these five people, whom you may have known well or virtually not at all, explain to you something about your life that you didn't know and teach you one thing so that you can at last rest and relax. As one of the people Eddie has to meet says to him, 'Each of us was in your life for a reason. You may not have known the reason at the time, and that is what Heaven is for. For understanding your life on earth.'

It's an intriguing idea that it takes five people to help us make sense of our yesterdays and it's an interesting exercise to ask yourself who these people might be for you. An alarming idea, isn't it, that one of the people who holds one of the keys to understanding your life may be someone you haven't even thought about for years. The idea, is not exactly new; many spiritual traditions have stories of people learning truths after death in order to lighten them so they can ascend into a heaven that becomes home. The Gospel story of the rich man and Lazarus is told by Jesus in that very same tradition, and it's worth taking a closer look.

Luke has a very clear interest in wealth and its dangers and his Gospel contains many stories of Jesus in which wealth is the focus, all placed together so that the point is made clearly. He notes that Jesus tells this particular story to the Pharisees, who mock Jesus – the Greek actually says, 'they turned up their noses against him'.

This is the only parable in which one of the characters in the story is given a name – Lazarus, which means 'God helps'. Interesting, isn't it? The poor and marginalized are often not given names, so they don't have an identity that impinges on our conscience. If you don't have a name then you are nobody. The radical Jesus is back! And this time it is the rich man who is not given a name. But it's almost as if we can't bear that, because in later centuries he was given one; it simply came from the first line of the parable as the Latin translated it: 'There was a certain rich man' – *homo quidam erat dives* – and that's what he became known as, Dives.

The rich man, we are told, likes his food, he's definitely an M&S man and not in the Co-op, and the word Jesus used for his eating is a crude word frequently used of a cow's munching – *chortazo*. He feasted a lot, and as usual in the culture, bread was used to wipe the grease from one's hands and was then thrown under the table. It's likely that the dogs ate the scraps that fell there. But in this story the unclean dogs also go and lick the sores of this poor man Lazarus who doesn't have the strength to shoo them away. In the Greek we are told that he had been 'thrown against the gate' of the rich man and the irony of the story is that the dogs are more aware of Lazarus's sores than the owner of the house who dresses in the finest purple from Savile Row.

Both men die and the rich man discovers that it is not enough to claim that you are of good religious stock, as he claims that Abraham is his father. He goes to Hades, which is to say the least uncomfortable – and again a twist of the story is that the one who did not show mercy now requests it of himself. He says that there is a great chasm between him and Lazarus after death, but actually it was always there: a chasm that he created by the way he chose to life his life. Now he asks that Lazarus help him out and become a sort of errand boy. What he wanted during his lifetime he wants reversed in the afterlife. He wants Lazarus to come close to him now.

We may be tempted to generalize 'the rich' since so few of us belong to that category and although the rich man is not named he's also not condemned for being rich but for his indifference and uncaring attitude to poor Lazarus outside his door who needed him. To free Lazarus from hunger you provide food. To free him from disease you provide doctors and medicine. To free him from the elements you provide him with clothing and shelter. But, asks Jesus, 'What about this rich man, how do you free him, free him from the prison of self and the uncaring attitude?' Answer: you provide opportunities for sharing his wealth. The Gospel text is clear: greed is concerned with getting, the gospel is concerned with giving. And if one's life is focused purely on getting you will never be satisfied, and bookshops will continue to have self-help next to get-rich-quick. We end up with lots to live with and little to live for.

There is one problem with this story as far as I'm concerned. It's actually hard to identify totally with either the rich man or Lazarus: difficult to picture oneself as so affluent or as catastrophically devastated. It may be then that we can more easily associate with the five brothers, those who still have the opportunity to be instructed and to see the beggar at our gates, to learn the lesson of giving not getting. The Church has often been nervous of the radical Jesus and ignored his teaching about money. Christians, for instance, get so worked up about sexuality and synods, which he never mentioned, and they divide over them, but you don't see the same passion from them – from us – about the things he did talk about and was passionate about. God forgive us for having tamed the words that carry life! It will not be enough to say afterwards, 'But I'm an Anglican! I believe in salvation by good taste alone!' So what? Did you help where you could? Perhaps you were cruel by keeping yourself to yourself?

In the parable, the rich man actually sees Lazarus only when in the afterlife. One of the prime dangers of comfort is that it does cause blindness; prosperity can limit our perspective and ignores distasteful shades that might disturb our enjoyment. Those five brothers need their sight back, need their sense back, and, says the storyteller, so do we.

36

Caravaggio

He has rescued us from the power of darkness and
transferred us into the kingdom of his beloved Son
Colossians 1.13

The author George Bernard Shaw was once asked which painting in the National Gallery he would save if there was a fire. 'The one nearest the door,' he replied.

One of my favourite exhibitions there explored Caravaggio and his influence on other artists. Caravaggio was born in Italy in 1571 and was only 39 when he died, yet in that short life he certainly made his name as one of the most talented and innovative of artists. He is also known for his rather tempestuous life: often arrested for carrying a sword in the street, taken to court for arguments and brawls, abusing the police and finally stabbing a rival who eventually died from his wound. He then went travelling, on the run really, ending up in Malta where again he was put in prison. He escaped but was later arrested in a port where his possessions were left on a ship that went sailing off without him, which he then pursued. Alone and probably suffering with malaria, he became feverish and died on his journey.

The National Gallery's exhibition displayed some fascinating works, many with religious themes, such as his late work of John the Baptist's severed head and the famous *Supper at Emmaus* with its beardless Jesus.

In one room of the exhibition you saw one important skill Caravaggio had that inspired others – his amazing technique of depicting light in darkness. Some of his paintings even appear almost black and white, as a candle throws its light onto faces and objects. In the *Supper at Emmaus*, the light of recognition when the two men suddenly realize who the bread-breaker is illuminates their faces. In his religious works the holy, whether Christ or his followers, throws an extraordinary light on the landscape which doesn't remove the darkness but does dispel its fear and danger.

Paul tells the Colossians: 'God has rescued us from the power of darkness and transferred us into the kingdom of his Son.' Rescued from the power of darkness – just as the light on a Caravaggio painting rescues the subjects, brings them into view, won't let them disappear into the dark background, but pours a light on them that seems then to ignite a light within them too.

If rescuing from darkness is the work of God, it is the work of the Church, and by that I don't mean popes and archbishops or synods or councils, I mean us. We are called to share in the work of rescuing children, men and women, from darkness. And there is darkness in this world, as we well know: lives are being ruined, diminished and even ended by militarized regimes, by poverty, by hunger, by terrorism, by hate crime, by an inability to imagine what it might be like to be someone other than us. The real danger is that we start to fail to notice. We get used to the TV pictures and to the language that the press and politicians and society at large begins to casually use: where the bombing of a school full of children is referred to as collateral damage; where someone fleeing for refuge, leaving home for their family's safety, becomes an immigrant; where degrading sexualized boasts about behaviour towards women is just locker talk; where God is praised as a head is cut from a body; where people trying to sleep outside on streets must have chosen to be there; and where upholding human rights based on a belief in equal human dignity is smirked at in pubs and papers, and churches too, unless of course they're talking about their own.

All this is increasing the darkness. Who will rescue the victims of it? Who, when society wants to push a person into a dark background out of sight, will shine a light and say, 'Don't you dare!' Who will rage with anger at the senseless death of children, at the discrimination and hate shown to the vulnerable, at the convenient casual categorization of human beings into first, second, third class citizens? Who will rescue from the darkness? The answer: the one who believes in God – not a God utilized to back a political campaign, not a God weaponized into a big version of our own prejudices, not a God who likes some more than others, but the God who loves equally all he has made: the God who gave us diversity though we tirelessly make division out of it.

We come here to worship with every bit of reverence and beauty we can muster. But we leave here with a clear brief – to bring hope and light to a world that is attracted to self-destruction. And we do this by anger and then courage, not anger and then indifference; not a shrug and maybe a prayer; but by energized, practical citizenship of the kingdom of God. The way Jesus preached about this kingdom implies that you can't get there, you have to be there. Joining God's mission, how will we join the rescue of those under the often plausible-sounding power of darkness? A letter, a protest, a better donation, a stirring of motivation for a better world – it can all be done or why else bother to pray? So, as St Paul writes: 'May you bear fruit in good work, may you be strong, may you be prepared to endure.'

37

Introducing Luke

I wrote about all that Jesus did and taught
Acts 1.1

It is said that some people bring happiness wherever they go and other people bring happiness whenever they go. Perhaps it's too frightening a thought to ask which we are! However, four of the Church's saints are called evangelists; based on the Greek root, this literally means that they are bearers of good news, carriers of hope. We know these evangelists as Matthew, Mark, Luke and John but we don't need to feel ashamed if we don't really know much more than that about them. That's why the Church gives us feast days for them, asking us to learn about those who have inspired the Church in the past and continue to encourage us today. And today it is Luke's turn. So, who was he and why do we celebrate him?

Whatever else he was, Luke was an author; over 25 per cent of the whole New Testament is written by him. Luke did not just write the Gospel we know in his name, he also wrote the first book you find after the Gospels called the Acts of the Apostles. This was his volume two. His volume one was the Gospel that tells the story of Jesus, then Acts tells us the story of the first disciples and the early Church after Jesus' earthly life in order to show how Jesus remained present when he was no longer with them physically.

We don't know exactly when Luke wrote these two documents. All we can say is that it was sometime between AD 75 and 130; most scholars think about AD 85. And we don't really know where he wrote them either. We don't know much about him. There is a tradition that he was a doctor and also a tradition that he was an artist: some icons and paintings portray him painting the portrait of Mary the mother of Jesus. It is easy to see why this image came to be, because it is only in Luke's Gospel that we hear about Mary the woman, and her Magnificat song, and find a focus on her in the infancy narrative. One thing we are fairly sure of is that Luke accompanied St Paul on his missionary journeys. He was almost certainly a Gentile although he obviously knew the Jewish Scriptures very well. Some people think that there is a connection between Luke and the city of Antioch, that he was writing under the patronage of a man called Theophilus, addressed as 'your Excellency', to whom the two works are addressed. His is the only Gospel where the author obviously writes himself into the text. But although Theophilus may have commissioned the work, or at least have been the first recipient of it, the Gospel is obviously intended for others to read too. It is very much written out of faith for faith, aimed at putting onto paper what had so inspired those first men and women whose lives had changed because of Jesus Christ.

I say Luke was an author, but he was more than that. He was a good author. He wrote in a high style Greek, not like some others who seem to have picked up Greek, but as one who is natural with the language, using it elegantly and with refinement. Ernest Renan called Luke's Gospel 'the most beautiful book ever written'.

Now when you read all the four Gospels a number of stories overlap, but Luke has many that are found only in his Gospel, and they are some of the most loved and moving stories of all. Only in Luke do we find the Good Samaritan, Martha and Mary, the Rich Fool, the Prodigal Son, Dives and Lazarus, the Pharisee and the Publican, the Good Thief, and the Disciples on the road to Emmaus. Imagine a Christian faith without these. As I mention these stories, you might begin to do what biblical scholars do to earn their salaries.

They look at the work of the author to see what themes he especially wanted to bring out to his readers, what ideas, what stresses and priorities he seems to have. With Luke they are fairly clear.

First, Luke is very wary of money. He is constantly using his collected material to show what bad effects wealth and comfort can have on the soul, so ingrained that those who are affected don't know. 'He has put down the mighty from their seat and exalted the poor, the rich he has sent empty away,' sings Mary (words found only in Luke), and then all the way through we see how those who don't have to worry about their lives end up not worrying about anybody's life: only Luke tells the story of the man in fine purple robes who passes by the beggar at his gate. Luke also seems to dislike any systems, religious or political, that come between God and the poor of the earth. The religious Pharisee, writes Luke, prays pompously and the publican can't even face himself; only the publican goes home in relationship with God.

Second, Luke continually stresses the mercy and compassion of God and the need for us to reflect the mercy we receive ourselves. The son makes a mess of life and decides to go back home and his dad is already down the street with his arms open. The problem is, hints Luke, that Christians, instead of being like that dad, tend to live like the brother who stayed at home, grumpy, resentful and lacking in grace and generosity. Likewise, it is a nasty foreigner, a Samaritan, who proves neighbour to the man beaten up. We know what the priests do: walk on the other side. Jesus' statement after telling this story in Luke is directed at whom? Well, a rich man of course: 'go and do likewise'; and you feel that this is Luke's continual invitation to his readers. He is open about our experience of guilt, our need of forgiveness and the radical open-arm-ness of God. Don't let these stories fall flat in you, let them be fruitions, hatching a newness in you, a mercy reflective of Christ. It is with very good reason that

Dante called Luke, '*il scriba della gentilezza di Chriso*', the scribe of the kindness of Christ.

And third, Luke stresses the work and continual presence of the Holy Spirit in our lives and especially in those who are on the fringes, considered outcasts. Not only the poor but foreigners, tax collectors, publicans, and women (always looking after Jesus and with him to the end, when it is they, not the men, who believe the resurrection!) – these are the heroes of Luke's Gospel, they are the blessed, the ones in whom the Holy Spirit finds it easy to live because there is so much room. It is not the religiously secure that seem to allow God space in Luke's Gospel. If you are satisfied with where you are you close yourself down to new opportunities and transformation. Luke was warning, and still warns us, about the dangers of tribe and religion, the way they can insulate us against the need of our neighbours. Compassion should overrule code. We find the Spirit moving in all the events of Luke's story, challenging and comforting in equal measure.

So, this is the man we celebrate – quite a man and not as distant, perhaps, as we might have first thought. At the end of his Gospel is the beautiful story of the confused disciples on the road to Emmaus who suddenly recognize Jesus in the breaking of bread. As they recognize him he disappears from view. It is a moving and profound truth that Luke did with those early Christian friends what we are here to do 2,000 years later, to break bread and listen to the Jesus story, so that our hearts might burn within us and we might go and do likewise in the name of the one we call Lord. 'Inasmuch', writes Luke at the very start of his Gospel, 'as many have undertaken to compile a narrative of the things that have been accomplished among us, just as they were delivered to us by those who from the very beginning were eyewitnesses and ministers of the word, it seemed good to me also, having followed all things closely for some time past, to write an orderly account for you, most excellent Theophilus, that you may know the truth concerning the things of which you have been informed.' Amen and thank you, most excellent Luke.

38

Useful Mark

Get Mark and bring him with you,
for he is useful in my ministry.
2 Timothy 4.11

Some years ago the actor Alec McCowen toured the country with his complete recitation of the Gospel of St Mark. It was a wonderful feat of memory and I remember being in the theatre listening to St Mark's story very carefully and differently because we only usually hear or read it in small sections. It was a great evening but I did think it a bit strange to break for a choc ice immediately after the Transfiguration, occurring as it does right in the middle of the Gospel.

I said just now that I listened differently. It is a fact that human beings hear and read things in different ways. If you picked up a book of Shakespeare sonnets you would engage differently with them than if they were Nigella's latest recipes or one of those impossible 'how to put it together' manuals from Ikea. Our word Bible comes from *biblia*, meaning books. In other words, it is not one book but a library, a wide collection of texts containing an enormous variety of writings in it: poems and hymns, proverbs and wise sayings, ancient history and mythology, visions, letters and, most importantly for Christians, four Gospels, accounts of Jesus' life and teachings written sometime between 40 and 100 years after his birth.

The man we celebrate today is the author of the earliest, we think, of those Gospels. As an author Mark wrote in a very specific way, designed to make you and me hear richly: that is, he was seeking to educate the soul not just the mind.

His faith was speaking to our faith through his creativity. What we have in this Gospel (a word we get from the Old English 'Godspell', meaning good message) from Mark is not a history book such as Mary Beard might write about ancient Rome. Nor is it an exciting but fictitious story like Harry Potter. It is an account of Jesus' life and speech, historically based but shaped imaginatively by faith and passion so that we can understand the depth of this man Jesus' significance both then and now. When we try and speak of the things that matter most – how much we love someone or miss them or what we believe deep within – we move beyond our usual literal use of words and call on every possible style, vocabulary and metaphor to get across what we must communicate so you get a glimpse of my heart and belief. That is what Mark does when he sets about writing his Gospel, a form of biography from an ancient world.

We don't know a great deal about Mark. Some believe he was a companion of St Peter and that he wrote this Gospel in Rome. Others think it might have been written in that currently sadly damaged country of Syria. Mark may have ended up in Alexandria, and for this reason he is held in great veneration by the Coptic Church of Egypt. Whatever the truth, he was a very early Christian. Scholars tend to think Mark's Gospel was written sometime between AD 60 and 80. He wrote in Greek, although it's a bit B– compared to Luke's or John's A+. And it would appear, through his use of a lot of Latinisms, that he was writing to a non-Jewish audience, a community of early Christians who were probably undergoing severe suffering. Mark spends half his Gospel on the darkness and pain of the suffering of Jesus – was this his way of encouraging them and showing them that their Lord understood what they were bearing?

One thing you note, especially when you hear the Gospel read in one sitting, is the speed of the text. Mark uses the phrase 'and immediately' nearly 40 times. St Mark's symbol is a lion and his Jesus comes onto the stage of the world with a roar. There is no nativity story in Mark – Christmas would be very different if we only had Mark's Gospel – instead he begins at the River Jordan with Jesus, who he says is a carpenter – the only evangelist to tell us this. Jesus is then baptized, distilled in the desert, and then he starts an urgent ministry of calling people back to God and showing in amazing ways how God loves, heals and rescues human lives that let him. All the way through the Gospel a question hangs over everything – who is this man? Can you work it out? Instead of spelling things out in ways that might be easily misunderstood, Mark presents an account of Jesus that is full of parables, riddles, misunderstandings and secrecy.

When Peter, right in the centre of the Gospel, does say that Jesus is the Messiah he is told to be silent, and a shadow then falls across the Gospel as the journey is made to Jerusalem and to his death. For this second half of the Gospel God is silent. Jesus dies with a cry to the God who seems to have gone and yet Mark tells us God had never been closer; he lets us know that the veil that separated God from his people in the Temple split as Jesus died. This has made one scholar of the Gospel, Richard Burridge, summarize Mark's Jesus: 'No one knew where he came from; no one knows where he has gone; and not many understood him when he was here – an enigmatic figure whose power was realized in suffering and whose kingship was proclaimed in death.' In the same spirit, Mark's account of the resurrection is perplexing. Only eight verses long, we get no appearance of Jesus himself, just some messenger saying he has been raised. Then the Gospel ends abruptly with women running away saying nothing because they are frightened. This wasn't good enough for some scholars, and an additional ending was given to the Gospel at a later stage – you can find it usually tagged on at the end in your Bibles.

It is clear that when later Gospel writers came to create their own narratives for different places and audiences, they had Mark's account in front of them and used a lot of it. It is equally clear that they also felt his account needed a bit of help, a bit more clarity and smoothing over. Mark is often raw, punchy, strangely beguiling, but too open-ended for some. For me, his is the Gospel that asks us to engage seriously with who this man Jesus is for us – someone we like reading about and admire, or the one we choose to follow even to death if we had to? It is the Gospel that shows that spiritually there will be a lot of misunderstandings on the way, betrayals and let-downs, but that, as T. S. Eliot said, we can be thankful that darkness reminds us of light. The silence of God, rather than the bullying or hectoring of God, is often how he gets closer and pushes our contours into spiritual growth. It is a Gospel of passion, poetry and parable, of a Messiah who suffers. It is a Gospel full of followers who don't get it, of people who live through the greatest things but miss the meaning, of faith being found where it shouldn't be and not being found where it should. It is a Gospel that teaches that faith ultimately runs into an unknown future with only 'Don't be afraid' in our ears for hope. But this is a Gospel that teaches us to trust in God's fidelity, not ours. This is a Gospel for me because this all sounds pretty recognizable – in me and around me.

Great St Mark, for showing us these things from your faith and artistry, for helping us hear richly in our souls and for encouraging us when we trip up or can't make sense, we thank you this day named in your honour.

39

Black Dogs

Out of the depths I cry to you, O Lord.
Psalm 130.1

People are sometimes surprised when I tell them that one of my favourite novelists is Ian McEwan. 'But he's so dark and eerie,' they say, 'he should be called Ian Macabre.' True, but what I admire him for is constant exploration of our privacies, the private reasons for things, the other story, the chaotic and shadowed truths that lurk beneath our polite handshakes, coughs and kisses. What binds all McEwan's books together is their power to unseat our moral certainties and sap our confidence in the clarity of quick judgements. His is the art of unease, the scalpel-slicing art of playing havoc with the preconceived. He cuts the ground from under himself, and in the process of course from under us as well. He is very much in the tradition of Graham Greene.

Common to most of McEwan's writing is his interest in the complexities of the human will and human need. In his Booker prize-winning book *Amsterdam*, we discover that a Conservative MP has a penchant for wearing women's clothing, and looking at the posing glamour-puss, outside the parliament chamber now, and photographed in the privacy of his home, the author reflects:

We know so little about each other. We lie mostly sub-merged, like ice floes, with our visible social selves projecting only cool and white. Here was a rare sight below the waves, of a man's privacy and turmoil, of his dignity upended by the overpowering necessity of pure fantasy, pure thought, by the irreducible human element – mind. (p. 74)

McEwan is an atheist. He is not as militant and evangelical in his atheism as Christopher Hitchens or Richard Dawkins, but he does not believe in God. The book I want to reflect on here, while not his best and not one that typifies the early darkness he was known for, is I think one that both atheists and believers ought to read because of this same art of unease that paper-cuts both groups.

Black Dogs was published in 1992. It was preceded by *The Innocent*, which ends with its hero foreseeing the fall of the Berlin Wall and an end to the barbarities its existence sustained. In *Black Dogs* we find the narrator travelling to Berlin with his father-in-law to join the jubilant crowds and watch the wall's collapse. In the festive air something else is brewing, though. At Checkpoint Charlie they become entangled in an ugly scene in which a young Turkish immigrant with a red flag is set upon by neo-Nazi skinheads, while middle-class citizens in suits observe the assault with ill-disguised satisfaction. The incident confirms the vanity of any simple-minded, sentimental hopes the visitors might have harboured. As the monument to the defeat and division of Nazi Germany topples, a vicious new generation of racists emerges to take up the fascist torch, and a terrible question emerges: what if the event that seemed to mark the victory of reason and popular democracy turns out to hatch something completely other? A question we seem to be living with.

This is the anxiety at the heart of the book: the fear that far from having left the apocalyptic horrors of two world wars behind we may be *en route* to reliving them, because the human drives that fuelled them have merely been suppressed and may never be eradicated. The forces of darkness, symbolized by the ominous creatures of the title, 'will return to haunt us, somewhere in Europe, in another time' (this is the last line of the book). Black dogs, of course, whether at the foot of Dürer's *Melancholia*, named by Johnson and Churchill for depression, or let loose by Artemis on mortals and devouring the unburied Greek heroes, have mythic qualities that remind us of the animal in us, that which bites, dismembers, tears and threatens. The dogs are the pervasive ever-present force that might leap into action at any time.

In *Black Dogs* McEwan stages the crisis into which his beliefs have been thrown and takes stock of what writing fiction entails. The contending viewpoints are embodied in the three main characters: the narrator, Jeremy, and his wife's parents, Bernard and June Tremaine. Jeremy's preface to his memoir of the couple, which furnishes the main substance of the novel, spells out the nature of the positions competing for the author's allegiance: 'Rationalist and mystic, commissar and yogi, joiner and abstainer, scientist and intuitionist, Bernard and June are the extremities, the twin poles along whose slippery axis my own unbelief slithers and never comes to rest' (p. 19).

For Bernard, the rational scientific humanist who left the Communist Party after Hungary in 1956 and became a Labour MP, it is human beings who inscribe on reality whatever intelligibility it yields; we make things the way they are, and we can change them for better or worse by changing the way we think and behave as individuals and communities. For June, however, a momentous encounter with two gargantuan black dogs while on honeymoon in France in 1946 has been enough to convince her that divinity shapes our ends, and that our lives should be devoted to cultivating its presence within us and resisting the incursions of its opposite, the pure malevolence manifest in the demonic hounds she fought off that day: 'I met evil and discovered God,' she says (p. 60).

From the standpoint of June, the soul is the battlefield on which a universal spiritual war is perpetually waged, and the revolutionary politics to which she too had subscribed before her revelation are a fatal delusion, an evasion of the deeper truths of being and the more taxing obligations of the human heart.

June's vision strikes a chord with her son-in-law. With the Checkpoint Charlie incident still fresh in his mind, he finds it hard to shake off her belief in an ineradicable taste for evil lurking in individuals and nations, an appetite 'no amount of social theory could account for' (p. 172). Fortunately, June maintains, to pit against this 'we have within us an infinite resource, a potential for a higher state of being, a goodness' and what she terms 'the healing power of love'. But it is at this point that her biographer's sympathy departs in quest of Bernard's disabusing antidote, marshalling its aversion to 'those clarion calls to love, to improve, to yield up the defensible core of selfhood and see it dissolve in the warm milk of universal love and goodness. It is the kind of talk that makes me blush. I wince for those who speak this way. I don't see it, I don't believe it' (p. 60).

Jeremy's mind shuttles back and forth between these two creeds; each strikes him by turns as banal, self-deceiving claptrap or urgent wisdom of global relevance, commanding unqualified assent. Listening to the two voices haranguing each other inside his head, he winds up paralysed, as so many of us are today, terminally stumped: 'Each proposition blocked the one before, or was blocked by the one that followed. It was a self-cancelling argument, a multiplication of zeros, and I could not make it stop' (p. 119f.). Like Bernard and June themselves, who have lived apart despite loving one another for most of their married lives, the stances wrangling inside the narrator's skull are doomed to remain wedded yet unreconciled.

I find Jeremy fascinating and somewhat haunting, almost a personification of present culture and politics. He stalks the lives of his surrogate parents, perhaps because of what he calls his 'irreducible sense of childish unbelonging', but makes a troubling discovery about himself:

> I discovered that the emotional void, the feeling of belonging nowhere and to no one that had afflicted me between the ages of eight and thirty-seven had an important intellectual consequence: I had no attachments, I believed in nothing. It was not that I was a doubter, or that I had armed myself with the useful scepticism of a rational curiosity, or that I saw all arguments from all sides; there was simply no good cause, no enduring principle, no fundamental idea which I could identify, no transcendent entity whose existence I could truthfully, passionately or quietly assert. (p. 18)

Like many of us, he has no home for his mind or heart. His words are spectators, never committed or participating, in the values and beliefs he discusses. And yet the trouble is, he also doesn't quite believe his disbelief.

In his preface, Jeremy makes a brave stab at stating an ultimate creed that escapes the clutch of what these dogs intimate: 'I would be false to my own experience if I did not declare my belief in the possibility of love transforming and redeeming a life' (p. 20). But what about the other side of the scales? This novel peers into an abyss. McEwan dissects with the ruthlessness of a child pulling the wings off a butterfly: 'I never had any doubts about it,' concludes Jeremy, 'at some level you remain an orphan for life' (p. 10). At the end of the day McEwan can only assure us that all we have is the fleeting respite of the stories we tell ourselves, the fictions we concoct to feed our hunger for sense. And so his omnivorous art of unease prowls on.

Is all this un-Christian, atheistic, not suitable for the children? Well, for me, McEwan simply takes us out of the shallows and explores the heartlands and confusions of a psalm-like territory of emotion and pain: God in the puzzle not the solution. This work is a challenge as to what we believe and why, asking what we mean by salvation and stopping us buying into that travesty of bumper-sticker theology that fakes authenticity. No, only out of the depths do I cry to you, O Lord. Lord, hear my voice.

40

Light on Snow

The Lord is my light and my salvation; whom shall I fear?
Psalm 27.1

It is the wrong question to ask of one's faith, 'What can I get out of this?', and it is the wrong question to ask of a book. Much of our reading today is consumerist, information focused, promiscuous scanning, fast reading trying to obtain facts and quick clarity. In contrast, say scholars, the reading that was typical in medieval Europe was quite different. It has been called lecturature, that is, reading that is also composition. As you read so you, the reader, are composed: your thinking, emotional and active life is changed and built on. By your close reading, ingestion, rumination, so a translation and creation takes place within you. Your conversation can be evidenced in the marginalia you mark next to the words. George Steiner famously reflected on Chardin's painting of the reading philosopher where the reader is literally dressed for the occasion of reading, not meeting the book casually but with almost a courtly display towards the text in front of him. This is an encounter and exchange. Both the book and the reader are read. Two worlds are being explored. The conclusion for the believer is that God so loved the world that he gave us stories.

With this in mind, I chose for this sermon series on writers a rather unlikely novelist – Anita Shreve. I chose her because she is a popular writer and, to the likes of some, perhaps a too little 'Richard and Judy' in her popularity. I also chose her because she is, I believe, a flawed writer. There is usually one character in her novels not properly developed, and there is often some dislocation in the narrative voice of her books. However, Shreve is a great story-teller and a story-teller unafraid to explore those emotions and situations that hurt. We cannot read her as a consumer. Loss, loneliness, betrayal, heartbreak – life is not for beginners in the Shreve world. As a Christian and as a priest, I am called to understand if I am to minister among people who bear such things. I can draw on my own experiences, of course, but I need help not to force the other's hurt into a box of my shape. Likewise, as a pastor, it is vital not to add insight to injury. You never help a person by simply telling them what's wrong and feeling better yourself for your diagnosis. The pastor has to take a bigger risk and, like the close reader of a book, open oneself to be changed by the encounter with the one who is hurting, risking being opened to your own hurt.

In her 2004 book *Light on Snow* we find a 12-year-old girl, Nicky, living with her father in a remote house out in the New Hampshire countryside. A road accident has killed Nicky's mother and baby sister, and her father would like to live in his grief like a hermit but knows in his heart that 12-year-olds need many things that the world has to offer. Then, one afternoon before Christmas, just as the light begins to fade, Nicky and her father find a newborn baby wrapped in a bloody sleeping bag in the heavy snow in the woods. They move heaven and earth to save the baby's life: getting the baby eventually to the hospital. For a moment this drama brings Nicky and her father together but afterwards the pair start to fall back into their old ways – tiptoeing carefully around each other, fearing to speak the name of their grief, pretending at normality. Until, that is, a pretty young woman comes knocking on their door – forcing all three of them to question motives and look into each other's hearts.

The story is told with crisp, understated prose, the simplicity of the style allowing its emotional depth. We see Nicky's growing perception of the world she is about to enter and the adults who inhabit it. She is learning the ways in which human hearts seek to heal themselves. She is learning that adults are not at their best when on their best behaviour. She is learning about the frozen sea of the soul that can lie beneath our politeness or silence. She is learning that so often in our meetings we capture the shadows not the substance of another person, fearing what they reflect of us. We find in this book personal tragedies colliding and the complexity of relationships this brings about. Who looks after whom? Who the child, who the mother, who the father? Love is greedy when it is starved. What happens to these roles when grief strikes and yet life goes on? Shreve shows the duality of the human spirit – frighteningly frail but immensely strong. She is learning that freedom is what we do with what has been done to us.

There is a lot of falling snow in Shreve's book, as the title suggests. When I lived in Copenhagen we occasionally used to get heavy snowfalls and it was amazing the effect it had. You had to work out what you really had to do – did you have to go out or not? The traffic virtually stopped and everything fell quiet. You were aware of yourself, your crunching shoes, your visible breath, your tingling fingers. People had to come together too – cars got stuck and needed people to push, people went round to their elderly neighbours to make sure they had food, roads had to be cleared by the street's residents.

I've said in the past that I think Lent is a snowfall in the soul: becoming aware of yourself in a fresh way, you discern what is vital and what isn't. Shreve's book similarly pours snow onto our manic, distracted lives, and calls us back to the stillness and pain at the heart of our short lives. But the book is called *Light on Snow*, and it is true that there is anticipation in this book, a promise of possible redemption, for the tragedies lie in the past and the movement is towards hope. The story of Nicky is of a fractured child, growing and regaining herself by seeking to name and recognize the wounds. 'The Lord is my light and my salvation,' the ancient poet dared to believe. Like God, the author in this book is always present but never seen, flickering and hinting a meaning within our turned pages: yes, casting light on snow, a gentle encouragement to defrost.

41

The 10th Anniversary of 9/11

'Blessed are the peacemakers'
Matthew 5.9

Like many people who were in New York in September 2001 on that initially bright and sunny morning, I have been left with very deep memories, some of which I wish I could forget. I remember too being on one of the first flights out of JFK airport a week or so later and seeing from the air the still smouldering remains of the towers and the nearly two million tons of rubble and debris that would take nine months to clear. And as the plane turned towards the ocean I realized I didn't want to go home. I felt I was deserting, flying away from so much need at a time when people needed people.

This reluctance to go home was very common on the day of the terrorist crimes itself. Those rescued from the buildings knew of friends still trapped. To go home felt a betrayal of their friendship, of all the days shared together. The emergency services personnel and hospital staff worked and worked to the point of collapse and still didn't want to go home – there was more to do, there were colleagues missing, lives were still held in the balance. The Mayor of New York at the end of his day returned to Ground Zero; he needed to be with his people. His home was with them. And there were of course the anxious families, longing to hear news of the person they loved, and the bereaved who had to go home, or had to stay at home, which felt like being trapped in a prison of pain, absence being the unbearable presence. In each, it was the protective desire to find and be with the one you would do anything for and end the cruel distance between you both. For those caught up in those indescribable hours this was not a day to go home. What would you do there? Who would you be? What would you eventually have to face? On that day 2,977 people were never given the opportunity to go home, including among them, if I may name just one, Robert Eaton, a former chorister of St Paul's who was working in the World Trade Center that morning.

Ten years later, in a changed world, we are back at home. Indeed for many it has been in our homes, among those we love most, that some healing begins to take place. Whereas our bodies often do quite a lot to heal themselves, human hearts are not so skilful. They need to be loved back into life and I know for many this is a day to thank those who have helped make the last ten years possible for them.

Together, then, we do something today that is both painful and courageous – we remember. And we do so not out of sentimentality or show but because human remembrance has life-giving reserves that are urgently needed if we are to do more than just survive as individuals and as a society. To remember helps us re-member, put ourselves together again, placing ourselves in some proper proportion, relearning what makes humanity human.

One of the roles of a church or cathedral is to enable people to remember. Today we do so, in a long tradition here, with American friends; and also with the British and other families of lost loved ones, with many people from around the world who have been affected by the 9/11 attacks and other similar tragedies. Many that September day were humbled by the courage of the firefighters, 343 of them losing their lives. It is right then that we also recall today the 20th anniversary of the Firefighters Memorial Trust, naming our gratitude for the passionate commitment of those who guarded all our cities, and indeed St Paul's, during the Blitz, and in the years since, giving their lives on active duty. It makes us proud to be alongside so many serving and retired firefighters here now.

Please know: we all salute you today for the service you give, day in and day out, to save lives in danger.

There has been much talk recently of a broken society and of the fault-lines that run through many of our communities. But we need also to see and name what we remember today – loved ones lost, but all the sacrifices for good, the working togetherness, the commitment to the unknown stranger, the desire to help the wounded and fragile, the faith communities' shared pastoral work, the courage to stop a plane destroying lives at the very cost of your own – all this, that we remember today, teaches us what we know already deep down but so unhappily ignore: that we are incomplete when we are self-absorbed. You can argue that life is survival of the fittest, but one day you will ask: fit for what? Many people, often invisible, live lives that don't break society but give society a soul. These lives were spoken about by Christ on a mountain when, against the tiring spirit of frenetic competition, he spoke of the blessed ones being the humble, those with some mercy in them, those who carry and share peace, those who hunger to see what is right be established, those who mourn and have experienced loss, those who know their need of God. And in a world where the high cost of our freedom is risk and pain, he also taught that no one has greater love than this: to lay down one's life for one's friends.

If this all sounds unattainable or even untrue, then just remember why all those people wouldn't go home that day. They knew that life demanded more of them and that their own life was recovered in responding to that demand.

We therefore dare to say that today we remember with hope, remember for the future, remember to live as those who died would want us to live. As men and women and children, the invitation that lies in this remembrance is to see that our relationships matter more than anything else and that we should treasure them and each other with everything we have. So much will urge you to go a different way: it really needs a revolution of the spirit like that preached about on that mountain. God's gift to us is our being. Our gift to him is who we become. It was Churchill who said that we make a living by what we earn but we make a life by what we give. As a society it means translating this priority of love into the priorities of justice and equity. It means supporting the vulnerable, all those who live and work peaceably and those who serve the common good. I don't know if all this will make a big society; more importantly, it will be a society with its soul back.

When this service has ended, we will all go home. We will have remembered with love and pride those whose lives were taken away and that part of our lives that went with them. We will have remembered those who made sacrifices in and beyond duty. And if we remember with hope, then all that they were to us and all that was so clearly seen on that day, not the brokenness of a society but its very pulse and life, will be our inspiration. And later today, when silence is kept by the families of the lost – to remember – in Grosvenor Square, even if there are some who will seek to disturb them, they will never be able to take away or shake what we ultimately celebrate today – the resilience and beauty of love and of the lives built on it. Where we remember this, there will always be hope.

42

The Patronal Festival of St James', West Hampstead

James and John, the sons of Zebedee, came forward
Mark 10.35

Some of you will know the story of the holy rabbi who went to the men's barber for a haircut. At the end, he went to pay but the barber wouldn't accept his money. 'No, Rabbi,' he said, 'I never take money from the clergy.' And the following morning when the barber got to work there on the steps of his shop was a bag of delicious, fresh bagels. The following day a Catholic priest went for a haircut. At the end the barber wouldn't accept any money. 'No, Father,' said the barber, 'I never take money from the clergy.' And the following morning, there on the steps the barber found a large bottle of whisky. The following day an Anglican vicar went to have his hair cut. At the end the barber refused his money. 'No, Reverend,' he said, 'I never take money from the clergy.' And the following morning, there on the steps the barber found an enormous queue of Anglican vicars.

Now there's something unnervingly accurate about this story! And, of course, it plays to the popular perception that religious people are often just in it for themselves. And often we are. Your patron saint, St James, we are told in the Gospels, wanted to ensure he got one of the best seats in the kingdom of God, and elsewhere we learn he got so hacked off that people in a town weren't as impressed with Jesus as he was that he thinks about asking God to kill them all with an angry zap from heaven. So, although we don't know much about St James, we do know this: Jesus will have spent a lot of time with him, gently but relentlessly showing him another way, correcting him, slowly helping him to see that nothing true can ever be said about God from a defensive, insecure or selfish place inside us.

It's obvious to me that you, as people of St James, have been learning over the last years the same lessons from the same Lord. Years ago this part of London was known as the 'West End' and in 1812 it was said to be so quiet here that you could hear the cannons at Waterloo – and I'm not talking about the station. There were only 200 or so residents here in those days. Times have changed and one of the many things I am grateful for is that you, as a church, have taken those changes seriously to see how best you can respond as people of Christian faith. Many in the Church talk as if we are just about being loyal to the past – and making tradition fresh is our calling – but our real vocation is to be loyal to the future, that we might help the kingdom come on earth as it is in the humility of heaven.

One of the things that has changed obviously in this locality is the size of the population. In fact, that's why this church was built in the first place – to serve an increasing number of residents. And what I briefly want to do is to look at just three of those residents, who lived very near to your church here, to see how I think they would have been very proud of their local church as you try today to listen to Jesus Christ, just as James did.

The first local resident is the poet T. S. Eliot. He lived for two years in Compayne Gardens in the early twentieth century, after he married his wife whose family lived there. Eliot was a person who, like a lighthouse, flashed a strong light onto who we have become as human beings. He believed that we are living buried lives, that we need defrosting back into something worthy of the name 'human'. Listen to him as he observes:

... the strained time-ridden faces
Distracted from distraction by distraction
Filled with fancies and empty of meaning
Tumid apathy with no concentration
Men and bits of paper, whirled by the cold wind
That blows before and after time,
Wind in and out of unwholesome lungs
... this twittering world.
(*Four Quartets*)

We are people in exile, Eliot thought, and we need to begin a spiritual adventure of picking up the compass to find that great harbour of love, God, where all our loose ends can find their mooring. God is the 'still point of the turning world' and that's why it is absolutely right that you say very clearly that worship and prayer are your lifeblood here. I'm from Shropshire originally and there are a lot of sheep in Shropshire and at the back of my grandmother's house I often see Tom, who's a shepherd. A few years ago I saw him in the field carrying a real shepherd's crook. So I joked with him that my boss the bishop had one of those too. And I asked him if he really used it to reach out and hook naughty sheep with and haul them in. 'No,' he said. 'The best use for this is to stick it down firmly into the ground so that I can hold onto it so tight that I become still enough that the sheep learn to trust me.' That's where we endeavour to speak and live from: that rooted, authentic place of relationship with God. So, ultimately, being here now is not about information, lots of chat about God, it is about being made, about God not as an object but as the subject of our lives. Thank you, St James', for reminding us that in a twittering world, God is not the object of our knowledge but the cause of our wonder. Eliot asked, 'Where is the wisdom we have lost in knowledge and where is the knowledge we have lost in information?' Your dance here with God, wisdom forever ancient and forever fresh, must indeed always be your lifeblood: to be unafraid to reason and unashamed to adore.

Then, living a bit further away was Margaret Postgate Cole, one of the amazingly strong and campaigning women, many of them suffragettes, that this part of London has known over the last 100 years or so; all of them would have given Theresa May a run for her money. Cole lived in Parsifal Road and was a real advocate and champion in her day for comprehensive education. She wanted an education system that served the children of each locality, and that desire to ensure that churches too have a genuine will to serve the people of the parish, whoever they are, is another lesson you have learned with St James from Christ. Being in tune with the kingdom of God is not to stand with the great but to sit with the broken; for a Christian community to be most truly itself will mean it not being selfish. The spiritual adventure begins on the day when instead of being curved in on ourselves we partner, befriend, welcome the neighbour and especially the overlooked, the ones whose voices get ignored. Thank you for what you do for your local community and for reminding the Church that, at its best, Anglican life is never congregational but parochial, being alongside the people among whom God has placed you. Your mission? Seeing that God has given us a wonderful diversity and that division is what we so often tragically make of it, you are to call us back to the celebration of that diversity and to show the people of West Hampstead that God is the God of all of us and that love is for everyone.

And finally, the last local resident I want to remind you of, born in Cleve Road and living there for a number of years, is Nicholas Winton, who organized the rescue of 669 children, most of them Jewish, from Czechoslovakia on the eve of World War Two. Winton found homes for the children away from the Nazi tyranny and arranged for their safe passage to Britain at great cost and risk. The last group of 250, scheduled to leave Prague on 1 September 1939, were unable to depart. With Hitler's invasion of Poland on the same day, the war had begun; of the children due to leave on that train, only two survived the war. He told no one about this extraordinary rescue operation; the world found out about his work over 40 years later, in 1988. Well, I don't need to tell you about the world we are living in and the rise of populist politics that will always use quick clarity and easy scapegoats to secure more votes and a takeover of power. And I don't need to tell you either of those in our own day suffering hate crimes, discrimination, being made to feel ashamed and at risk for simply being who they are. You may not be organizing trains from Prague here, but St James' has made it clear that this is a home of safety and welcome for those against whom the currents of the political day blow, those currents often being felt in the Church as much as in the world. There come times in life when you realize that if you don't stand for something you will fall for anything.

There will always be a cost to being the challenger, the reminder, the one who keeps honesty in the arena, reminding us all that there are never 'swarms' of people, never true labels, never 'collateral damage' in war, never enemies better kept behind walls – there are only ever other human beings, created with all the dignity God can bestow, and in need of friends when the mood shifts against them or when they have lost everything. Thank you for helping many of those people, not least LGBT folk, to hold their heads high, high towards heaven so that they too can hear the voice: 'you are my child too, loved and cherished and for always'. We are afflicted in every way but not crushed, is the message of Paul. Amen. Christian people have helped the hate of discrimination towards LGBT people and others, even giving the world a language to do that hating in. It must be our responsibility to help undo what we contributed to. And you, with others, have taken this duty on yourself and many thank you for it. Nicholas Winton, like many who have been brave for a humane humanity, knew the words of Martin Luther King Jr:

Cowardice asks the question 'is it safe?'
Expediency asks the question 'is it politic?'
Vanity asks the question 'is it popular?'
But conscience asks the question 'is it right?'

So, it's a real joy to be here with you and to celebrate your life and Christian witness together. You live in the locality where Eliot saw the need for our roots to feel the rain of God; where Cole wanted everyone around us to benefit from that rain; and of Winton, where we see what a life looks like that knows that what we do to the least we do to the one who made us all.

You're not perfect, thank God. You have lots of cracks that grace can still pour through. You have lots more to learn, lots more to do, lots more to celebrate: but God is with you, and just as St James listened and was changed by the journey with his Lord, changed by love for love, so are you – God bless you. Stay loyal to God's future!

43

The Samuel Johnson Festival

With their mouths the godless
would destroy their neighbours,
but by knowledge the righteous are delivered.
Proverbs 11.9

'To be alive is so amazing,' said the American poet Emily Dickinson, 'there's hardly time for anything else.' I'm delighted to be here to help us celebrate a man I feel sure would have agreed.

The last time I came to Lichfield and into this amazing cathedral was 29 years ago when I was thinking through my own sense of vocation before going to see Bishop Keith Sutton who then sponsored me for training for priesthood. I grew up in this diocese of Lichfield and, like Samuel Johnson, was to make my way eventually to London. But also, like him (from his later mid-life onwards), I've always remembered and returned to this diocese with huge gratitude, and when I say to you how good it is to be here with you today, I hope you'll understand just how much I mean it.

My journey to London was a little easier than that of Johnson. He travelled in 1737 with his friend David Garrick, whom we also commemorate today in this 300th anniversary year of his birth, with, it's said, only one horse between them and taking about a week.

Now, Johnson and Garrick were two incredibly talented men, as the years would show, and history happily remembers them, whether by theatres, clubs, museums or societies founded in their celebration. But, why do we come here to Lichfield to remember them? What has a dictionary-maker and an actor got to do with a cathedral and the Christian faith? Well, I want to suggest, more than we might imagine. In fact, to remember them and their passions is, to my mind, pretty urgent.

They were both men of words. And today is a bad time for words. Listen to them all on the TV debates, social media, opinion columns: the first person to draw a breath is declared the listener. The danger is that words become cheapened, as disposable as anything else. They tend so often to be shaped for battle rather than for a density of suggestion that allows growth of minds and unlocking of hearts.

When Garrick began his management of Drury Lane theatre he asked Johnson to write a prologue for the opening night. Johnson decided to have a go at what he saw as the degeneration of English drama, but his words could equally apply to much of what we are living through. He refers to the pomp of show, the fact that declamation roars while passion sleeps, that virtue has had to flee under cover: 'Intrigue was plot, obscenity was wit. / Vice always found a sympathetic friend; / They pleased their age, and did not aim to mend.' Using words to control the world and others to your own advantage rather than using them to mend, build relationships, respect beauty, truth, a shared human dignity and justice – this was as concerning then as it is today.

Christians, of all people, should scrutinize language as it is used, be distrustful of quick and seductive clarity, remembering the spiritual truth that difficulty can be very important in a life, and cautious of a too-easy fluency. Christians are not interested so much in relevance as in resonance of words from which we can't retreat, words that seem to listen to us, words untainted by testosterone poisoning, with no chemical additives. We long for words that help us migrate to the things that matter.

So, there was Johnson, working away on his 2,300 pages, believing that dictionaries are the pedigree of nations because the character of our language defines us. As he worked he saw how language cannot be prescribed, but that like water, if it isn't fresh and moving it is stagnant and deathly. His dictionary is buried treasure, full of examples of how words have vitality in their movement and contexts. At great cost, the light he casts on all this was achieved through battling with a lot of inner darkness and, in his words, amid inconvenience and distraction, in sickness and sorrow. But this was the dictionary used by Keats and Wordsworth, Austen, George Eliot, Wollstonecraft, Bentham, Mill and Dickens. Its afterlife is present in the Constitution of the United States; lawyers there are still turning to it for its proper interpretation.

But as we know, it is more than a dictionary, it is a celebration of the loves, losses, quirks and curiosities of what he called the 'current of the world', the glory of this spiritual adventure called being alive. It is a work of literature in its own right. And at its heart is that belief that words and truth should be inseparable and beware those who think and act otherwise. Likewise Garrick, bringing the language of Shakespeare especially onto the stage and into lives, ensured that words were not two, three, four or a hundred steps removed from who we are, from our humanity, but were, scalpel-like, dissecting us, alerting us to ourselves so that language could ultimately recognize and illuminate life and never darken it. Language is there to help us to enjoy life, or to endure it.

Finally, Johnson was a Christian. Boswell tells us that 'religion was the predominant object of his thoughts'. Indeed, I wish he was still around as he often wrote sermons for his clergy friends. If you read his prayers and reflections you get a strong sense that he believed that God had given him a gift, his being, and that he was asked to give a gift back, his becoming, who he becomes. But he feels he makes a mess of this, he is lazy or distracted, paralysed from goodness and so in need of grace, of a God who gives much more than we ever deserve, a restorer of all our broken vows. Aware always of the tension between the face we live with and the face we die with, he was convinced that 'Christianity is the highest perfection of humanity', and this enriched and informed everything he ever wrote. And, I would claim, this instilled in him a reverence and care for language, knowing that words do indeed become flesh for good or for ill.

So, when I leave Lichfield in a little while and pick up my luggage – which he defines as 'anything of more bulk than value' – I shall have said my thank you to two people who more than ever should be remembered here, in a Christian church, thanking God for their lives of language and their language of life.

44

The 450th Anniversary of Highgate School

But wanting to justify himself, he asked Jesus,
'And who is my neighbour?'
Luke 10.29

I don't know if any of you have heard about a thing called the Pie of Knowledge. It is an attempt to describe your own knowledge of things in relation to all the knowledge in the universe by making a pie chart, like a sliced cake, cutting it into sections. The first slice of this Pie of Knowledge is made up of those things that you know you know (so, for example, this might be the plot of *Hamlet*, your mobile number, or how to make pancakes). Then there are the things you know you don't know (this may be a larger slice and may include nuclear physics, the mating rituals of the horsefly, the names of all the stars, or what this sermon is about). The third slice contains things you know but have forgotten (e.g. the French word for 'ear', your grandparents' phone number, the age of the headmaster). The fourth slice of the pie is very interesting: it represents the things you don't know you don't know (I can't give you examples here because that would mean I knew). The last slice is the things you think you know but really don't – your family or friends might be better able to identify these for you (e.g. what it was like to have been in Auschwitz, why my neighbour is like he is, the defence policy of the Green Party). Now which, I wonder, would your biggest slice of the cake be? The things you know you know, the things you know you don't know, the things you know but have forgotten, the things you don't know you don't know, or the things you think you know but really don't?

Let me help you. For all human beings, no matter how old we happen to be, the largest slice will be the things you don't know you don't know. This slice probably makes up 99.9 per cent of the cake. The total knowledge of our universe is so vast that the sum of all human knowledge is infinitesimally small by comparison. It's good to recognize the things we don't know. A lot of tears in life come from pretending otherwise. And the first thing a good education can do is place a longing in us to find out more, a deep-down passion and excitement to make the mind fresh again. But there's another role for education and that is to make us able to distil what we know and to understand the things that matter. A former teacher of this school, T. S. Eliot, once asked: 'Where is the wisdom we have lost in knowledge and where is the knowledge we have lost in information?'

The founder of the school, Roger Cholmeley, was a bit of a lad when he was younger. When he was at Lincoln's Inn he was fined for not attending lectures, for breaking down doors, for spending too much on wine (the two were probably related), for gambling with the Chaplain and for getting into debt. Later in life, old and now respectable, some men were brought before him to be disciplined. They knew of his past and appealed to him by reminding him that he too had once been a lad. His reply? 'Indeed in youth I was as you are now and I had friends like unto myself but not one of them came to a good end. Therefore follow not my example in youth but follow my counsel in age.' His school was an embodiment of this desire to distil life, our knowledge and experience, into something of worth for us but also for the common good.

A lot of religious people talk as if what really matters in life is what you know, getting your knowledge right and somehow being saved because you're right and others aren't, but

THE 450TH ANNIVERSARY OF HIGHGATE SCHOOL

the tradition of religious faith is very different – although in the Christian world there are many who seem to prefer a Church that is right to a Church that is loving. It seems to me that at the heart of Christian faith are two deep perceptions. The first is that God has given you a gift. It is your life. Your being. There is something gift-like, fragile but unique about you. And there is a gift we are asked to give back in return. Our becoming. Who we become as human beings. A good glimpse at how you're doing is to ask, who do people become in my presence, what do I make them become when they're with me? You'll get a snapshot of the sort of person who are turning into. Use that snapshot, if you don't like what you see, for some amendment.

The second perception of Christian faith is that the world has got it wrong. Living is not about spending money we don't have on things we don't want in order to impress people we don't like. Life is not behaving as if it is just survival of the fittest and not being able to say, OK, but fit for what? Human dignity is not established by going with the mindless indifferent crowd or just joining the noise of now, but about committing yourself to a purpose, values, to the things that matter. Jesus ended his story about a brave and kind man with a jolt: go and do the same. The truth is, if you don't stand for something in life you are going to fall for anything.

So if your education is only about information and not about formation, and if it is teaching you how to click a button on Google to get an immediate answer instead of teaching you to be very aware of the seduction of quick clarity, and to be cautious of the easy answer and the first perception, then complain tomorrow morning. From the very beginnings of your school, for your founders and bishops of London with them, education was more than gathering facts or a sausage factory for making another thoughtless consumer. It was to change consumers into citizens, and enable the whole person to be generously spirited, open to the new, and wise not just in what they know but in what they become. Cholmeley was buried 400 years ago just outside St Paul's. You will hear him turning if his school forgets these things.

A time of thanksgiving such as this is a time to make a resolution, to the years you have left and those you share them with – to make sure you're living a life and not just a competition. As Churchill said, you make a living by what you earn, but you make a life by what you give.

I'd like to end with a story in tribute to those 176 former pupils of Highgate School who were killed in World War Two, whose end in Europe we also remember 70 years ago this year. I was brought up by my grandparents. As a boy I knew my grandfather had flown in the Royal Air Force and he was a bit of a hero to me. But he never spoke about his experiences, except one day mentioning 'Dresden' and weeping. I didn't understand then but I do now. Some years ago I was asked to preach in the reconstructed Frauenkirche in Dresden. My grandfather was very much in my mind. On the way to the train station at the end of my visit the taxi driver asked me why I was in Dresden and I told him I had always wanted to come. 'Why?' he asked. I took a deep breath. 'Because my grandfather was a navigator of a Lancaster bomber and on 14 February 1945 I know he flew here as part of the bombing raid and he could never talk about it.' The man was quiet and then said: 'Ah, that was the night my mother was killed.' He pulled over and turned the engine off. He then turned round to me, put out his arm to me and said: 'And now we shake hands.'

That man, like me, knew the facts. He knew the horrors of that night, he had lived his loss, learned about the thousands dead. But he knew more. He had become wise. He knew how to make a full stop into a comma, how to interrupt revenge and make it into something more true. He taught me something that day and it is something that a school can celebrate: that we rightly ask what it might mean to be loyal to the past, but the more urgent question is, how can we be loyal to the future? And that is over to you and who you become: the things that you believe matter. God bless this school, and your education into the mystery and privilege of being human. Be loyal to your future. Your founder must have the last word: 'In youth I was as you are now ... follow not my example but follow my counsel.'

45

The Festival of Preaching

For all of us must appear before
the judgement seat of Christ
2 Corinthians 5.10

You've been asked to preach a sermon to a lot of people attending a conference on how to preach well and you've been given five minutes maximum. So, what are you going to say? Face it, you're a bit frightened. Every time you sat down to start writing it your heart started to beat quicker, and that's a bit uncomfortable.

Tell them why. Tell them that it wasn't that long ago that you had chest pain going up some stairs, that you ended up in the heart hospital having a lead put in your groin up into your heart, that the doctor turned the screen round and said: 'Take a look. You're a lucky man, Mr Oakley, you had about three months left.' Tell them how you looked at that screen, looking like a satnav of veins and arteries, and for the first time really realized you are a body, that although you live in your head, in words and ideas, you are a fragile, time-limited body, dependent on that strange, pulsing miracle on the screen over your head. Tell them how you asked the doctor if he would kindly stop talking and get on with it then, how he laughed and placed a tiny stent to open up the artery so that your blood could flow free, free and fast. Tell them how you had to look away from the monitor at that point, you wanted to live by faith and not by sight. You just hoped the doctor had the opposite view.

Tell them it was that day, after crying with relief that it looked as if you'd be OK, lying on the hospital bed, that you made some decisions. You decided to enter a civil partnership after having been fearful before of what it might do to your future ministry. That day, you didn't really care about that any more. You just wanted to acknowledge the love that has carried you through many years of your life, the person even now holding your hand in the recovery ward saying: 'It's OK. We're still here.' It was that day too, when he'd gone home, that I said to God in a voice I felt was actually me, that we were alone now and could we please start again? I see now that Paul too was working out stuff between his body and his longing for life, his longing to make sense of being a created body for a time but wanting the beyond. 'We must all appear before the judgement seat of Christ,' he says.

I felt I was there that night. It took a hospital bed to get me to see that the things that matter most in this world – love, relationship, connection, trust, wisdom – these are the things that increase as they are shared. The more you give of these the more you have. They are unlike wealth and power, there-fore, where if I win, you lose. In all the things that we know matter more than anything else, the truth is that if you win, I win too. Tell them in that sermon that it puzzles you why it took you so long to see it, that you had to be distilled, that now if you understand anything these days it's that this is the truth that Christian faith celebrates. Grace means receiving more than you deserve. It's what our world at the moment seems to lack.

You will have reached your five minutes, so end by telling them that months have passed and churchy stuff doesn't hold the same interest it once did, but say how when the doctors told you that you needed some repair work in your heart, you sensed that God agreed. And that it's still true: work in pro-gress, trying to make a life of love and courage. Being a priest still feels as if I'm trying to help other people have a relation-ship with God I only wish I had myself. But they might be surprised to know that you've at last begun to go back to the teachings of the One you made promises to once. And they sound different: the blessed ones being the humbled, those with some mercy in them, those who carry and share peace, those who hunger to see what is right and bring it about by facing their fears, those who mourn and have experienced loss, those who know their need of God. 'We want what is mortal to be swallowed up by life.' I think Paul understood. He knew that life is there to upset your beliefs sometimes.

Tell them you just know that when R. S. Thomas said that a poem is what reaches the intellect by way of the heart, you think he was speaking of God too, at least for you; that day your heart became the focus and you realized you wanted to love better: your partner, your family, your friends, even those you have yet to meet. And God. And God.

46

The 170th Anniversary of Bloomsbury Central Baptist Church

Therefore lift your drooping hands and strengthen
your weak knees, and make straight paths for your feet,
so that what is lame may not be put out of joint,
but rather be healed.
Hebrews 12.12–13

1848 was quite a year. Not only were revolutions taking place all across Europe, with nation states being created; not only did Marx and Engels publish the Communist Manifesto, a Californian gold rush take place, Wagner begin writing his *Ring* cycle; not only did W. G. Grace arrive in the world and Emily Brontë die, and electric light get exhibited for the first time in Trafalgar Square, but right at the end of it, in December, Bloomsbury Chapel was opened. Samuel Morton Peto had helped fund it, having made money building railways – not sure what he'd make of our railways today – and the first minister was William Brock. Brock wrote a Foundation statement and here is part of it:

In the year 1848 a spacious chapel was erected in Bloomsbury, for the worship of God and the preaching of the Gospel ... in the hope that in due time a congregation might be gathered within its walls; and that ultimately a church might be formed in connection with it, which recognizing no other Baptism but the immersion of professed believers, should welcome to its fellowship all followers of Christ; should observe the Lord's Supper every Lord's day and should co-operate with other churches of Christ in such works of faith and labours of love as are incumbent on all who love our Lord Jesus Christ.

That last statement, a commitment to work together with other churches, Brock took very seriously. Indeed, on Sunday mornings he walked down Gower Street with the then Rector of St George's Bloomsbury, Henry Montagu Villiers, and as they parted to go to their churches they exchanged a blessing. So, it's good and very much in the spirit of the foundations of your church for you to be so generous in inviting me as an Anglican to speak here on your 170th anniversary.

And, of course, I could now preach a sort of half-learned and nuanced sermon on the differences of our churches and a celebration of the richness of our diversity – but I believe the times are too urgent to indulge ourselves in this way because, 170 years later, we are living in a very different world. Your charge here is also mine, and that's enough – to preach the gospel.

Now another of your neighbours here is the British Museum and walking around there you'll see the statues and paintings of the old gods of Greece and Rome. And whereas so many today are dismissive of religion they fail to see that gods have moved into our own world unnoticed and they are so strong that we are blind to their power. There are many of these gods but let me mention quickly just four because this is the world we are to preach the gospel in.

The first is called Gloss, the goddess of beauty and sur- faces – a fickle being, incarnated in paper and adverts, a god so big she makes us all feel small and ugly. We are drawn by her siren voice but her perfection is impossible even for those who anoint themselves with her many sensuous creams and labels. She is cunning too – she makes humans confuse their wants with their needs and this leads to many tears. She teaches that life is survival of the fittest. Fit for what, she never reveals. She makes objects into people and people into objects, so in her adverts you can never work out if the man is having an affair with the woman or with the car. Gloss desecrates human beings and this quickly leads to them doing the same.

Obese is the god of gathering, of acquiring, who is never satisfied: happiness for him is having what you want not wanting what you have. And he always wants more even when bloated. Although people say he is seen on earth at the moment in the form of bankers, in fact he is found in most hearts that have forgotten that the best things in life are not things, and that there is a price to pay when everything has a price. He is related to that great god who makes us buy things we don't need called Ikea (mainly worshipped on a Saturday). Together they magic us into spending money we don't have on things we don't want in order to impress people we don't like. And because customers and consumers are always right, everything touched by his commercialism is changed in character and the values that have governed the meaning and purpose of goods are eroded all in the hope that storing up is the path to happiness. How Obese laughs as he magically allows money to turn us into people we would prefer not to be without us noticing.

Instantaneous is the goddess of now. She cannot wait. She must have fast cars, fast food, fast money, fast death. She is blind, never having the time to stop and see anything. She often gets into a mess because she never has the patience to listen to anyone either. She beckons people to live full lives but strangely leaves them feeling empty. She is afraid of people meeting face to face in case they discover the joys of wasting time together, and so she invents screens and devices that trick us into thinking we are communicating but actually they add to our loneliness. She seduces with easy answers, and hates ambiguity, relationship, poetry, faith, art.

And finally there is Punch, the god of violence and division.

If hate can be escalated he'll have a go – if they don't agree with you, lash out. If they're different, slap them down. If they're not in the majority, don't invite them. When in doubt, just punch them. Now obviously Punch is the creator of some computer games, street gangs, film directors and state leaders. Religious leaders are often drawn to his clarifying power too. But Punch can be a subtle god and can hide in the consensus of the middle classes, and his punch can be made not of a fist but of plausible, respectable, articulate words. Punch can be very charming as he drives around in his bandwagon. He can make you feel better even as society fragments around you. And he loves to play a little trick – he likes to make people yawn whenever the conversation turns to human responsibilities, refugees, the poor and marginalized, the environment and an endangered creation, equality, the danger of the market being its own morality – in fact, anything that Christians believe are very close to God's heart. Punch is making the world a place where if you are not at the table you are probably on the menu, a place where we can't trust the words of our leaders who campaign in graffiti and govern in tweets and who make us shrug our shoulders to think that everything is possible but nothing is true.

Let's not pretend, then, that we live in a God-free world. We are in a pandemonium. The question will always be which god you have chosen to follow or maybe which god has taken hold of you. The question will always be, where do you place your faith, your trust, where do you place your hope?

Who we become will depend on the gods we cling to because we begin to reflect what or who we worship, turning into people we would prefer not to be without really ever noticing.

Last Sunday in the Church of England we remembered John the Baptist and the prayer we said asked that according to his preaching we will say sorry for the way our lives get on bad tracks and we will constantly 'speak truth, boldly rebuke vice and patiently suffer for the truth's sake'. I'm guessing that no one walked home from the Jordan and shook John's hand, then, and said, 'Nice sermon, vicar,' before lunch. No. What happened instead is that they cut off his head, the place where his tongue lived, the place from where words came. They silenced him. He had appeared in the desert, a barren, dry, thirsty place that symbolizes the world we have created. And it's quietly indifferent and quietly desperate there. It had all become a desert of a life and here arrives John, like an air-raid siren, someone speaking again the language of God – someone who looks into the future and can see where it will all end and who reports back quickly before it's too late; someone who is urgently telling us to take a look at ourselves, admit where we've gone inhuman, telling us to uphold what is just and right and not always seek compromise. Someone who asks us for God's sake to be a citizen of the kingdom of love and not a consumer of the world of competition, con-suming away even the environment we live in and breathe, consuming away our hearts in envy, consuming away com-passion towards those who so need it in a hard life.

Anyone who tells you that belief in God shouldn't be mixed up with political consequences – well, show them John the Baptist, show them Martin Luther King, Archbishop Tutu, William Wilberforce, Elizabeth Fry, Dietrich Bonhoeffer, Edith Cavell, Janani Luwum, Esther John, Gene Robinson, and ask how they could speak the truth, rebuke injustice and evil and suffer for God without being political? They were following Christ, and if he was a man who just spoke about spiritual things with no threat to the establishment or status quo, why did they execute him?

Speaking for them all, Archbishop Tutu wrote, in *An African Prayerbook*:

I don't preach a social gospel; I preach the gospel, period. The gospel of our Lord Jesus Christ is concerned for the whole person. When people were hungry, Jesus didn't say: 'Now is that political, or social?' He said, 'I feed you.' Because the good news to a hungry person is bread. When you are ill, I heal you. If you are neutral in situations of injustice, you have chosen the side of the oppressor. If an elephant has its foot on the tail of a mouse and you say that you are neutral, the mouse will not appreciate your neutrality.

Those who dare to preach have to be brave. They invite the world to be reimagined. They are willing to sound sadly implausible as they push the words 'God', 'mystery', 'love' and 'eternity' back into a landscape that has very nearly lost the echoes. It is an intensely personal enterprise in an alarmingly public arena. And sometimes nothing can feel more urgent. So, as Hebrews 12.12–14 tells us: 'lift your drooping hands and strengthen your weak knees, and make straight paths for your feet and strive for peace and holiness.' Be shepherded here by Christ alone. Your first minister Brock wrote that 'every person who constitutes the Church is a fellow-helper to the truth'.

This church has a long and distinguished history of preaching God to a world confused and diminished, intent on self-harm and destruction. I have a feeling and a hope that this pulpit will be equally busy in the days that lie ahead. Because when presidents start saying, 'These aren't people they are animals' wanting to infest a country; when children are used as bargaining chips; when parliaments in European countries pass laws to imprison those who seek to help those looking for refuge; when judicial independence is removed in a Western nation; when interior ministers call for a cleansing and purification of his country, neighbourhood by neighbourhood; when another European country has to cancel its performances of *Billy Elliot* because a media campaign says it could turn children gay and promote deviance; when abuse and discrimination are just the way it goes, and in the Church as much as anywhere else; when states of emergency mean states of control and the imprisonments of lawyers, journalists and Amnesty workers; when human dignity is shrugged off and human rights are laughed at because we are not talking about mine; when we see that this is our world now, not in the 1930s but now, then this pulpit will be busy – because all this is contrary to the gospel, to the hope and the dream of God's kingdom for all people that this place was built to proclaim. I hope and pray it will be a fountain to draw the fresh water of a different way of being human. This pulpit is here to make Christians stand for something, not fall for anything. And we stand for love. Erich Fried's words seem fitting to end in celebration of a church where in 1917 your minister wrote in his pastoral letter: 'Let us escape from the failure of attempting only the possible.'

What is it?

It is madness
says reason
It is what it is
says love

It is unhappiness
says caution
It is nothing but pain
says fear
It has no future
says insight
It is what it is
says love

It is ridiculous
says pride

It is foolish
says caution
It is impossible
says experience
It is what it is
says love

47

The 60th Anniversary of the Accession of H.M. The Queen

you anoint my head with oil
Psalm 23.5

In describing what it was like as a small girl to watch the Queen's coronation on a neighbour's new television 60 years ago, one woman remembered the beautiful young princess standing in the abbey with such gorgeous robes and it looked, she said, as if she would float up to the roof at any moment and all these men kept handing her heavy things and even put something big on her head to stop her floating away.

Well, a year and a few months before, indeed 60 years to this very day, that young princess had been informed of the death of her beloved father. She was in Kenya, staying at an observation point watching wildlife, and the news was unexpected for her father, the king, was only 56. And she was only 25. She began almost immediately to write letters and messages apologizing for cancelling the rest of the trip and for upsetting people's plans. And so began a life of impeccable duty and one that we give thanks for in this jubilee year.

It is perhaps rather telling that these 60 years' service of Queen Elizabeth began in the Treetops rest-house on an observation platform in a giant fig tree. For she has been able ever since to look out in an extraordinary way on the events and players of world history. Her reign so far has spanned 12 British prime ministers, 12 American presidents and six popes. She has travelled farther and met more foreign leaders than all her predecessors put together, from Haile Selassie to

Emperor Hirohito, and 'personally met' it is estimated about four million people. During her reign a man has stepped onto the moon, the Berlin Wall was built and knocked down, the internet made its appearance, apartheid in South Africa ended, the DNA revolution in medicine took place. They have been an extraordinarily fast 60 years, with changes in society that no one could have imagined that day in Kenya, and it has been said that she has offered a still, small voice of calm through them.

She is the 40th monarch since William the Conqueror obtained the crown. In a world that is now shaped by personalities it is not perhaps usual to praise the qualities of continuity and consistency but it is exactly these strengths that the Queen brings. Governments come and go, we can kick them out when we wish to, but in all the upheaval and whirlwind of political frenzy the Queen offers a non-political stability and continuity that actually allows and helps change to occur. This is a head of state who shakes your hand not because she wants your vote or because you voted for her, but because she embodies a vocational leadership that stands above such cynicism. Hers is a public service: duty and not personal gratification or achievement. There is a cost to such an inclusive calling. And this is where I think the present Queen is quite remarkable, for she has shown more self-control and restraint in 60 years than most of us could manage in 60 minutes. She is never pulled into blurting out her personal thoughts every which way but remains an antidote to raw political power by embodying loyalty, service, the human touch and that quiet dignity on which true relationship and transformation are built. And that is why instead of address-ing rallies of supporters or calculating ways to win power, she will take time to meet and listen to and encourage and thank the forgotten, overlooked, the ordinary – giving them the respect they deserve, not as a photo opportunity – the Queen does not need photo opportunities – but because these are all her people whose interests she vowed to serve.

Those vows were made at her coronation, a Christian liturgy in which, at one point, she was anointed with oil that had been made by the royal apothecary Savory and Moore, containing ambergris, musk, orange, jasmine and rose water. After the singing of the *Veni Creator*, as at an ordination the Queen had oil placed on her hands, her heart and her head. The Archbishop then prayed.

A round orb with a cross set on top was handed to her, to remind her that the world, with its resources and riches, is subject to God. As from biblical times, the Queen was anointed, that is, set aside and strengthened with prayer, to serve her people with leadership, to reign over them not rule over them, to take up a call from God and from the people to make a personal sacrifice of putting self behind and placing the common good first. Today, in her message the Queen has committed herself to this task afresh: 'In this special year, as I dedicate myself anew to your service, I hope we will all be reminded of the power of togetherness and the convening strength of family, friendship and good neighbourliness, examples of which I have been fortunate to see throughout my reign.'

Four hundred years ago, our other Queen Elizabeth addressed her people in words that history has handed down to us as her Golden Speech. 'Though God hath raised me high,' she said, 'I count the glory of my Crown, that I have reigned with your loves.' The devotion, dedication and steadfastness of our Queen is both her service and her gift to us – and we in return today reaffirm that she reigns with our loves and with our thanks to her and to the God to whom she made her vow.

48

The 200th Anniversary of the Birth of Søren Kierkegaard

be doers of the word, and not merely hearers
who deceive themselves
James 1.22

I am delighted to join you today in celebrating and giving thanks for one of the most gifted, creative and provocative thinkers within the Western philosophical tradition and, as a man of Christian faith, someone who challenges and inspires us to think differently not just about human existence in general but about our own lives.

As I saw my name on the list of speakers for today alongside some of the world's greatest experts on Kierkegaard I felt as I think Pontius Pilate must feel about the Creed – delighted to get a mention but slightly unsure as to the role I'm actually playing. For I am here to preach, not lecture, and as a preacher very aware of Kierkegaard's criticisms of church preaching: not least that image of the gander high up in the pulpit who after the geese have waddled into the church each Sunday preaches about the glory of their wings. Every Sunday the geese listen to the sermon and waddle home, before returning the following Sunday for the same lofty speech about the use of their wings. Whenever one of them asked why no one actually flew anywhere, various geese responded with nuanced arguments about the dangers of what happens to those who actually attempt it. You will remember what Kierkegaard concluded:

The trouble is not that Christianity is not voiced ... but that it is voiced in such a way that the majority eventually think it utterly inconsequential ... Thus the highest and the holiest things make no impact whatsoever, but they are given sound and are listened to as something that now, God knows why, has become routine and habit like so much else.

So, no pressure then ... I just have to take comfort in those words of the late Quentin Crisp that if at first you don't succeed, failure may be your style.

Of course, what we are celebrating today is partly that voicing of Christianity that Kierkegaard did through his 27 large volumes of published and unpublished writing. I first came across some of those writings at school where my Religious Studies teacher was a great admirer of Kierkegaard and published several articles on him. As know-it-all students we found him gloomy, sexually screwed up, and a bit intense – although we liked his irony and attacks on established religion. University reintroduced me to him and since then the works of Kierkegaard have never been far away from my desk, and then, living in Copenhagen for three years, I found myself in the company of many other admirers who introduced me to things I had never seen or understood in his words, and for that I remain very grateful to Denmark.

So, if I may, I just want to give a very short personal response to what has meant so much over the years as I have tried to engage with this remarkable spiritual giant.

The first thing I have admired Kierkegaard for is his pilgrim nature: almost a pilgrim poet more than a fixed philosopher. Pilgrim and poet are two important words to faith as I see it. Pilgrim: in that although religion has a reputation for being there to answer questions, it tends to work more fruitfully when it instead questions answers. Faith's opposite is surely not doubt but certainty because arrival stops the journey and faith is a continual path in which all those little hard stops in our life are often painfully changed into commas, so that there is more to come, more to embrace and ultimately more to be thankful for. For those of us with faith it is our doubts that often hoe the ground, bringing dark but fresh soil to the top ready for some new planting. Faith is a pilgrimage of learning and unlearning, distrustful of the soundbite or easy summary. And because of this, poetry is also a vital word for faith, resisting the curse of literalism that simmers down life and sensibility. A poem is like a stone thrown into a pool with all the ripples slowly but relentlessly making their way to your shore, lapping over your shorelines and shifting your sands. Kierkegaard's writing, his imagery, has these ripples for me, ceaselessly and richly giving food to an imagination that is seeking to be faithful not only to the past but also to the future.

So, Kierkegaard the pilgrim is an encouragement to me first, just by who he is: a poetic explorer on a spiritual adventure, waking us up out of that tussle we live of asking too much or too little of ourselves rather than being freed in spirit, to start over continually, aware of illusions but not to become disillusioned. Like Jacob he struggled and fought and limped and questioned, so that God might break in and, as he says, pick the lock of self-love. And all this because although we change and must change, God does not.

Second, I am grateful for Kierkegaard's descent into humanity, into human will and intentionality, into what we make of ourselves, and what is made of and by us, without us even noticing most of the time. Nothing is less self-evident than the self and he exposes this. His writing is a spiritually serious scrutiny of whether we are recognizable to ourselves. It should not surprise me that it therefore was in my mid-life that Kierkegaard's exposé of our sleepwalking through life in comfort and caution and often in the name of Christ struck me. Mid-life: that traditional period when we discover, as the great mythologist Joseph Campbell once said that: 'We spend the first 35 or 40 years of our existence climbing a tall ladder in order to finally reach the top of a building; then, once we're on the roof, we realize it's the wrong building.'

His exploration of us being opaque, a riddle to ourselves, passionately self-promoting – Kierkegaard pushes us to see what happens to the dimensions of our being and awareness when instead of taking out insurance we make a leap. He understands the shifting complexity of experience in the here and now but instead of shrugging his shoulders about it just being like that, he reminds us that we have a will, potential, a struggle to be and to be alive by a relationship with the ground of our being. The great question to ask ourselves is who do people become in my presence, what do I make people into when they are with me? Kierkegaard understands the answers there might be to that question and why. The meaning of Christianity for him is the meaning it has for his life, his one life, its choices, relationships, words spoken, actions done. He reminds a tweeting, broadcasting culture that actually truth is never merely consoling, but hard, angular and ultimately liberating, not as an entertainment but as a practice. When I think of Kierkegaard I think of those words in the poem 'Song' by R. S. Thomas, that Jesus Christ:

Comes to us in his weakness,
But with a sharp song.

As the letter of James urges, we are to be doers not hearers. It is not the sound of the noisiest or just good PR. We cannot possess the truth, the truth must possess us – and God is to be feared not because he is out to get us, vindictive, angry, but because he is real. Our masks, of the culture, of the crowd, of the composed, that eat into our faces and all our fantasies and daily fraud, buckle in the light of eternity and of God who sustains it. For me he is the great preacher of present possibility.

Finally, I am drawn to Kierkegaard for his continual, unapologetic emphasis on love. Of course, I love his irony and vicious attacks on the Church's institution and personnel. He knew that just because you are in a church it doesn't make you a Christian, just as being in a garage doesn't necessarily make you a car. Bishop's mitres in the Church of England are often like candle snuffs that put out the flame. So, I like his realism and challenge and courage. But it is love that he comes back to, as indeed should Christianity if it is to be true to itself. As John of the Cross reminds us, it is what, at the evening of life we will be judged on. And he did not believe in a cruel, capricious God whose love we somehow have to buy but in a God whose love, he said, is 'never a love whose ardour cools because of the ungrateful human race or my ingratitude'. So we must set out to love not with what he terms that preferential love that caters to our preferences, our friends and lovers, but with that commanded love that serves the needs of others regardless of who they are. Loving your neighbour in English translation doesn't quite get it, as 'neigh', or near, suggests we should love those near and dear to us. The German *naechste* is better: loving the next one to come through the door – anyone, everyone. We love by trying to make better.

It strikes me that the man we celebrate today, even in his short life, was so rooted in the true demands of Christian faith, rooted in the soil of Nazareth, that slowly but surely we begin to see that he is to be trusted. A Church in danger of becoming the bland leading the bland needs him urgently, recalling us as pilgrims, as people with a will and who make choices as to who we become, and as people whose compass must always be love. For Kierkegaard, almighty creative God, 'tusen tak!'

49

The 50th Anniversary of the Sexual Offences Act, 1967

to let the oppressed go free
Luke 4.18

I was at a conference not too long ago at which the speaker began by saying: 'As I don't know many of you here I asked for a list of you all, broken down by age and sex. But,' he said, 'as I look at you now I can see that most of you have indeed been broken down by age and sex.' I didn't dare to use this line on you this morning. As I look out at you now I see people in this church who have a much greater right to stand where I am and speak to you: people I have looked up to over the years as being brave for love, people who are still being the sort of people I want to be when I grow up – challenging abuses and discriminations against human dignity and identity and, at the same time, often suffering those same abuses themselves, healing through their scars. And if you remember nothing else of anything I say today, please remember this: everyone in this world who believes that human energy is wasted and poisoned every time it tries to discourage or stop human loving, everyone who believes that we all get a little closer to being human when we can love, freely and without fear, these people, thank you for everything you have given for helping to make this world a place that can begin to feel more like home, a world that wants us. Many who were on the same journey are no longer with us and we honour them here today. But now too in our own time I see you all here, ambassadors for human love, and in many dangerous, unforgiving places. Thank you and thanks be to God.

Fifty years ago, then, just down the road in Parliament a vote was being taken about sexual intimacy. As preparation I read the Hansard accounts of the debates that followed the Wolfenden Report and led to the 1967 Bill. It is not a pretty read. Much of the language is full of hate, ignorance and ominous warnings about slippery slopes and the end of the world. It's all being repeated, of course, in many parts of our world still. When I hear of those who were convicted in the past now being able to seek a pardon I think it should be the state that seeks a pardon for the abuse and injury it perpetrated. We know that what eventually resulted in 1967 was a partial decriminalization, shadowed by an age limit that reflected a fear of predatory men and an obvious attempt to make gay men invisible, out of sight in a locked private room. Lesbians and bisexuals, of course, were already invisible in that they weren't even talked about. As I read the scripts I was struck by how a largely white, male and heterosexual group had such confidence in talking about something they quite clearly did not know much about, maintaining a social order that suited them well. I saw how people who had probably in their lives only ever been challenged about their views, who had never been rejected by anyone just because of who they are; people who knew about guilt (saying or doing something wrong) but knew virtually nothing about shame (being something wrong); and how these probably well-meaning people, as they sat on green or red benches, held in a balance the lives, the convictions, the suicides, the depressions and the potential freedom, happiness, integration and authenticities of those they debated – all in their hands. Church debates in our own day can be very similar. We are here to say, literally, thank God that they made the first and important step in the right direction. Others had to follow to ensure more changes came in the cause of justice and equality, not least for trans men and women. That work continues.

I remember the first time I ever went on a protest march. As a recently arrived student I joined others outside this church and we made our way to Downing Street to protest about Section 28. I remember a man wearing a badge saying 'Why assume I'm straight?' A loving friend gently took him aside and assured him that nobody had. But it's salutary to recall that you only have to be 14 or younger to not have lived in this country with laws that outlawed the promotion of homosexuality and 'pretended family relationships', and that still had the gross indecency law, the same law that ensured Oscar Wilde stared at the prison door movingly displayed at Tate Britain's Queer British Art exhibition.

In those post-Wolfenden debates the Church of England's voice was, of course, present. In 1957 Archbishop Fisher reminded his listeners that 'There is a sacred realm of privacy ... into which the law, generally speaking, must not intrude. This is a principle of the utmost importance for the preservation of human freedom, self-respect and responsibility.' His successor, Michael Ramsey, took up the theme, highlighting that it is 'totalitarian states that define their own sense of sin and then make it a crime,' and that if you do consider homosexual intimacy to be sinful then this did not, and should not, mean it be made criminal. Other church leaders agreed. Some of them, along with a few bishops, joined the Homosexual Law Reform Society and got, I'm sure, many green ink letters for it. It's good to be reminded that sometimes the Church can actually be a little ahead of public opinion, something it might be easy to forget.

Let me take you back to the first words of the oldest Gospel we have. A man called John has been attracting attention by reminding people that we have been given a gift called our being and we are asked to give a gift back in return called our becoming, who we become. We therefore might need a bit of wash, some amendments, to start again and renew the purpose of our lives. So he preached by a river, the Jordan. People had come out to take a look and listen. Lots of gossip and intrigue on the shore of the river, I have no doubt. Then his cousin turns up, Joshua or Jesus, and asks to be freshened, 'baptized', in the water. He gets pushed under the surface. You can only hear you under there, your own heart beating; all the noise from the shore, the opinions, the dogmas, the criticisms and empty chatter, gets drowned out. It's just him for a second or two and then, pulled out, he takes a deep breath of fresh air, a start to a newer life. We are told that he then hears a voice. Not from the shore but from heaven. This is the one voice that matters and it is tells him, 'You are mine, I love you, you make me happy.' Jesus then goes into a wilderness where all the empty voices come back at him, tempting and torturing his mind, trying to simmer him down out of the dignity he discovered by the water. In that desert he is learning to live up to the voice that matters, and not live down to the ones that don't, those that want to suffocate him. In Matthew's account, this included the devil endlessly quoting the Bible at him.

This story is in the deepest heartland of Christian faith. For Christians, because of this story, water is thicker than blood. Baptism is where we hear the truth of who we are. Because of this story all the Scriptures are read to hear that love between the lines and any interpretation of the Bible where you cannot hear that voice of love is not to be trusted. When people use a text without some context it's usually a pretext for something else. The Bible is a record of people struggling, with mixed results, to believe that God loves people that I find it hard to. The truth of the waterside is the voice from God to each and every one: 'I've made you, look, you're beautiful, you make me happy, now, don't forget this even when they act like animals against you, even when you act like an animal because you're frightened.' When the Church believes this it works hard to ensure that in the ark every weird and wonderful creature has to budge up a bit to make a bit more space in the hay for another one. Christian spirituality is the business of speaking up for others. And in a world like ours at the moment when if you're not at the table you're probably on the menu, that's an important calling, and a tragic failure if we don't live up to it. And when a country believes similar things, that each of its citizens is wanted and full of potential for a shared life, that we need to listen to each other in order to have the imagination to understand how it is to be someone else, when their reality is allowed to become part of my reality, then, yes, a nation becomes, a world becomes, not a wilderness but a place to live and breathe together.

Christians have many different views on issues that affect LGBT+ men and women. That's no secret. We read the next alarming or mildly encouraging instalment every day. But we are here today to remember specifically the costs of criminalization and that, as people of faith or as allies of different faiths or none, we have a lot of work to do for brothers and sisters suffering those costs, invasions of their dignity, as we sit here now. Many of them are in Commonwealth nations, some of them in fear not just of prison, humiliation, loss of family, job, self-respect but their very life itself. In 2016 the Primates of the global Anglican Communion reaffirmed their rejection of criminal sanctions against gay people. Senior Roman Catholic leaders have condemned the notion that gay people are criminals. The Methodist Church and many others are clear too. So there needs to be a much louder ecumenical pressure placed on the leaders and governments of the over 70 countries, both from the Church here and in those nations where its voice is very influential, to uphold the dignity, freedom and beauty of God's gay men and women, made by God and loved. The Church needs to take responsibility to help change a state of affairs that it helped bring about. Apologies are not enough if they don't take the form of change. Sympathy is always easier than justice – and I'm a bit fed up with it. I hope that one thing to come out of this service will be to translate its faith into an action, campaigning loudly and clearly, encouraging those struggling for change in unsafe circumstances and, also, demanding that our government renew its commitment to LGBT+ asylum seekers. While LGBT+ people in our world are still criminalized none of us is truly free. The wild beasts are still at work. They need angels to minister to them. That's you.

So, a day of sorrow, a day of gratitude and a day of resilience, anger and hope. A day to celebrate the love heard at the Jordan, that trying to stop God loving his people is like trying to stop a waterfall being wet. It's a day to see that the enemies are, as always, silence, secrecy, hypocrisy, shame and fear; and that it's never as simple as just 'speaking truth to power' because power often already knows the truth but can't admit it. We are here to be saved from that patience that makes us patient with anything less than freedom and justice for all God's people.

When Jesus returned from the desert, committed now to the only voice that mattered, he gave his first sermon: 'The Spirit of the Lord is upon me, because he has anointed me to preach good news to the poor. He has sent me to proclaim release to the imprisoned … to set at liberty those who are oppressed …'

If this is our dream, let's pause here and think of those who have gone before, but then hold our heads up as we make for the door, hearing the same voice from heaven, and ready again, in Christ's name, to make the dream come true.

50

Matthew Shepard, Rest in Peace

'If the world hates you'
John 15.18

If the world hates you.

Matthew Shepard was an American student at the University of Wyoming. Twenty years ago, at the age of 21, he went out for a drink and at the end of the evening two men offered to give him a ride home. They did not take him home. Instead they drove him to a remote, rural area. They hit him on the head, continuously, with blunt weapons, tortured him and then tied him to a fence. They left him there in freezing temperatures. Matt was there for 18 hours in a coma until a cyclist saw him and thought he was a scarecrow. Getting closer he saw a young man with his face completely covered in blood except for where his tears had partially cleansed his cheeks.

Matt was taken to hospital. His injuries were too severe for him to be operated on. He lay on life support for six days until, at 12.53 am on 12 October 1998, he was pronounced dead.

If the world hates you.

Matt Shepard was gay. His killers knew that. His killers didn't like that. Other people didn't like that. At Matt's funeral, his parents had to walk past members of the Westboro Baptist church holding placards that said 'Matt's in hell' and 'God hates fags'. His parents decided not to bury Matt's ashes anywhere because they believed that his grave would be defaced. They kept Matt's remains at home. Until last Friday.

On Friday, at Washington Cathedral, 20 years later, his ashes were carried into a full cathedral. At a service full of lament and colour, sadness and resolve, Matt's remains were finally laid to rest in the cathedral. The preacher at the service was Bishop Gene Robinson, the first openly gay bishop in the Episcopal Church, who recalled the day, five years after Matt's death, when he was consecrated as a bishop. He was in the vestry putting on a bullet-proof vest, as the FBI had told him he must because there had been too many death threats received, when a note arrived from Matt's mother. 'I know Matt is smiling down on you today,' it said. Bishop Gene kept it with him through the service. The vest had to remain on for several months.

If the world hates you.

Today is the Feast of St Simon and St Jude. We know very little about St Jude. In fact, all we really know is who he wasn't. He was 'Judas not Iscariot', says the Gospel of John. Because his name continued to recall his traitor namesake, there was initially a resistance to invoking Jude's prayers. So he became 'the saint of last resort'. But eventually 'the saint of last resort' became 'the patron saint of lost causes' and in that capacity countless desperate people still turn to him seeking his intercession.

Two days after Matt Shepard's final interment, and just after National Hate Crime Week, St Jude is a good saint to remember. He was the man known for what he wasn't. He was not Iscariot. Matt was known for not being straight. The list of people who know they are often seen for what they aren't is long – defined by not being white, not being clever, not being physically the same, not being British or sporty or Western, not quite fitting in, not being like the local majority. We label people as not being like us. They are other. This can then mean that they are not really human as we are and so we can do anything we like to them. The violence can take many forms: from isolation, teasing, bullying to mental, spiritual and physical abuse, to leaving someone tied to a fence with their skull broken or nailed to two pieces of wood with thorns pushed into their face.

If the world hates you.

The Gospel tells us today that we do not belong to a hating world. We belong to God. Jude may be known here for who he isn't but God knows Jude for who he is and God loves him like anything. You may sit here now knowing what others think of you because of what you aren't. But you sit here with God who knows exactly all you are and can yet be and loves you for it. Matt was an Anglican and wonderfully his church loved him and showed him that no matter whatever happens, no matter whatever anybody says or thinks, the love of God for him was certain and true and for ever, even beyond death. At the end of his sermon the bishop, in tears, said that he had three things to say to Matt in that cathedral: 'Gently rest in peace here. You are safe now. Welcome home.'

The bishop then told the congregation that if they thought being there at the service was enough, they had misunderstood. They were there to be transformed by what had happened and to leave the place to make sure these things don't happen, and that means working out how you will vote, what you need to challenge, what you need to support, who you need to look at again, who you need to be alongside, and seeing too who you need to help you get through life, people who will remind you of the love of God for you. If you don't stand for something you might fall for anything. Don't fall, not us in here, with a belief in God-given dignity of all, for God's sake. Stand and stand up now for an end to this hate and for a love of people in all their whacky and wonderful difference, a love for people who need that love at the moment because there's too much hate towards others who don't fit in with my world going on.

If the world hates you ... I have chosen you out of the world.

The policewoman who was called out to the scene of Matt's attack says that as she approached the fence she saw something next to his body. It was a deer, lying quietly beside him. It looked as if it had been there all night long. She said the deer saw her, stood up, looked her right in the eyes and then ran away. 'That was the good Lord, no doubt, no doubt in my mind,' she said in her report, 'that was the good Lord.'

References and Further Reading

Albom, Mitch, *The Five People You Meet in Heaven* (London: Sphere, 2004).

Auden, W. H., *Collected Longer Poems* (London: Faber, 1968).

Brown, David, *God and Mystery in Words* (Oxford: Oxford University Press, 2011).

Brueggeman, Walter, *Interrupting Silence: God's Command to Speak Out* (London: Hodder & Stoughton, 2018).

Burridge, Richard A., *Four Gospels, One Jesus* (London: SPCK, 1994).

Carlisle, Clare, *Philosopher of the Heart: The Restless Life of Søren Kierkegaard* (London: Allen Lane, 2019).

Ciardi, John, 'Nothing is really hard but to be real', *Person to Person [poems]* (New Brunswick, NJ: Rutgers University Press, 1964).

Cope, Wendy, *Two Cures for Love* (London: Faber, 2009). Used by permission of the author and Faber & Faber Ltd.

Eliot, T. S., *Four Quartets* (London: Faber, 2001).

Eliot, T. S., *Murder in the Cathedral* (London: Faber, 1965).

Fallada, Hans, *Alone in Berlin* (London: Penguin, 2009).

Fried, Erich, *Love Poems* (Richmond, Surrey: Alma Classics, 2012).

Hughes, Gerard, *God of Surprises* (London: Darton, Longman and Todd, 1986).

James, Eric, *Time to Speak: 40 sermons* (London: SPCK, 1997).

James, Eric, *Word Over All: 40 sermons 1985–91* (London: SPCK, 1992).

Kierkegaard, Søren, *The Essential Kierkegaard* (Princeton, NJ: Princeton University Press, 2000).

Ladinsky, David, *I Heard God Laughing: Poems of Hope and Joy* (New York: Penguin, 2006).

Lessing, Doris, *Documents Relating to the Sentimental Agents in the Volyen Empire* (London: Jonathan Cape, 1983).

MacCulloch, Diarmaid, *The Reformation* (London: Penguin, 2004).

Mayne, Michael, *Dust that Dreams of Glory: Reflections on Lent and Holy Week* (Norwich: Canterbury Press, 2017).

McEwan, Ian, *Amsterdam* (London: Jonathan Cape, 1998).

McEwan, Ian, *Black Dogs* (London: Picador, 1992).

Oakley, Mark, *The Splash of Words* (Norwich: Canterbury Press, 2016).

Orwell, George, *1984* (London: Penguin, 2000).

Sassoon, Siegfried, *Sherston's Progress* (London: Faber, 1936).

Shreve, Anita, *Light on Snow* (London: Abacus, 2004).

Taylor, Barbara Brown, *The Preaching Life: Living out your Vocation* (Norwich: Canterbury Press, 2013).

Thomas, Dylan, interview in *New Verse*, 11 October 1934.

Thomas, Dylan, 'Poetic Manifesto' in *The Texas Quarterly*, IV.4 (1961).

Thomas, R. S., *Collected Poems 1945–1990* (London: Orion Books, 1993).

Tutu, Desmond, *An African Prayer Book* (London: Hodder & Stoughton, 1995).

Williams, Harry, *True Wilderness* (London: Continuum, 1994).

Williams, Rowan, *Open to Judgement* (London: Darton, Longman and Todd, 2014).

Acknowledgements of Sources

Wendy Cope, 'Names', in *Two Cures for Love* (Faber, 2009).

T. S. Eliot, *Four Quartets* (Faber, 2001).

Erich Fried, 'What it is', in *Love Poems*, trs. Stuart Hood (Calder Publications, 1991, reprint edition Alma Classics, 2012).

Daniel Ladinsky, *I Heard God Laughing, Poems of Hope and Joy, Renderings of Hafiz* (Penguin Books, 1996 and 2006). Used by permission of the author.

R. S. Thomas, 'Song', 'H'm' and 'Pilgrimages', in *Collected Poems 1945–1990* (Orion Group, 2012).

R. S. Thomas, 'Don't ask me', in *Residues* (Bloodaxe Books, 2002).

Index of Biblical Texts